Praise for
BETWEEN TW

G000130627

"If you doubt it's possible for one imag █████████████
Genesis to Revelation, then you need t█
Between Two Trees. There isn't another bo█████████████████████
in its pioneering methodology and in its brilliance of presentation. I
found myself completely absorbed and provoked by my own missed
readings of the Scriptures."

"Through theological reflection poised with poetic flare, Shane Wood
admirably explores the trials and triumphs of a world united to death
yet wooed by a tender father to return home. This book challenges our
understanding of the problem of Eden and enhances the revelation of
the depths of God's solution in Jesus—union with God. Reading *Between
Two Trees*, you will be deeply enriched, tenderly called, and masterfully
guided into the transformative power of the incarnate Christ."

"A professor of mine once told me I could not understand either the
apostle Paul or the Bible until I understood the potency of death. He
said Paul was a 'thanatologist,' which means one who studies death. That
professor was right, but very few—until Shane Wood's excellent, playful,
and poetic exploration of the Bible's thanatology—have let the specter
of death emerge in furious force in their theology. *Between Two Trees* is
a splendid entrance into the heart of Christian theology."

"The Bible tells a huge story, one big enough to embrace, empower, and
transform everyone's story. This book unpacks that huge story as well
as any I have ever read. I am so grateful to Shane Wood for giving the
church such an insightful and helpful way to understand God's big story.
Between Two Trees will help us grasp a better narrative and help us transform our own stories into better tales of redemption."

"The Bible opens with a tree, and it closes with a tree. In between, we find an epic tale of God's love for us. Shane Wood knows the metanarrative of Scripture like few others, but what is more important is that he lives its principles every day. He trusts the author who writes the story and the gardener who cares for his creation. Be sure to read *Between Two Trees* and nurture the fruit within."

—Kyle Idleman, author of *Not a Fan* and *Don't Give Up*

"How do you tell the story of humanity as portrayed in the Bible and make it both riveting and relevant with fresh twists around every bend? Shane Wood has accomplished just that. Part autobiography, part theology, and part narrative of the story of every human being, we laugh, cry, agonize, and end with great hope as we see the story of creation, fall, redemption, and consummation with fresh eyes. A delight to read."

—Craig L. Blomberg, Distinguished Professor of New Testament, Denver Seminary

"*Between Two Trees* is a contemplative and passionate work that explains in a scholarly yet accessible manner the personal transformation we can all have by knowing Christ Jesus. Shane Wood brilliantly challenges us to cling to hope, love, and life, even while we are in the middle of struggle, strife, and division. I highly recommend *Between Two Trees* as a guide for your spiritual journey."

—Dave Ferguson, Lead Pastor, Community Christian Church, Naperville, IL, and author of *Finding Your Way Back to God* and *Starting Over*

"Simultaneously honest confession and wise counsel, Shane Wood's *Between Two Trees* invites us to contemplate life in terms of union and transformation. Anyone looking for new perspectives on old questions about faith and life, about sin and death and God, about being fully human, will be enriched by this book. It guides us toward living between the trees of creation and new creation in light of the tree in the middle: the cross of Jesus."

—Michael J. Gorman, Raymond E. Brown Professor of Biblical Studies and Theology, St. Mary's Seminary & University

"Shane Wood understands that our life of union with God has been reduced to a simple transaction: confess Jesus, get heaven someday. He opens our eyes to the drama and mystery of God's ardent longing for humanity and our eager response to this relentless love."

—Jan Johnson, author of *Invitation to the Jesus Life* and *Meeting God in Scripture*

"Shane Wood steers our heads and hearts to the final pages of the Bible and helps us better understand God's blueprint for a transformed creation. The work of Jesus has changed, is changing, and will change the sinful world we live in, and that includes our sin-saturated lives. *Between Two Trees* will help you bridge the gap between who you are and who you most long to be."

—Jon Weece, Lead Follower, Southland Christian Church, Lexington, KY, and author of *Jesus Prom* and *Me Too*

"Only a few authors compel me to immediately read anything they write. Dr. Shane Wood is one of those authors. I know of no finer scholar who truly embodies what it means to love God and love people. You'll find his reasoning to be well thought-out, God-centered, and full of grace. I'm grateful for the insight, encouragement, and conviction that Shane's work has brought to my life. I know you'll experience the same as well."

—Caleb Kaltenbach, author of *Messy Grace* and *God of Tomorrow*

"In his own inimitable style, which can only be described as theological poetry, Dr. Wood manages to bridge the breadth of the Bible by rooting the grand narrative in a tangible metaphor of two trees. This simplified template of God's metanarrative helps us get our hands around the entirety of the Bible. We owe a debt to Dr. Wood for allowing us to see with prophetic clarity God's heart as well as our own."

—Mark Moore, Teaching Pastor, Christ's Church of the Valley, Phoenix, AZ, and author of *The Chronological Life of Christ* and *Kenotic Politics*

"Shane Wood penetrates the surface of the biblical story to reveal how God's original creation went wrong and how it will be restored. Wood shows that the redemption God offers is nothing less than restoration of the Eden ideal, which is at the heart of our deepest longings. With fresh insight, Shane Wood explores and explains the fear, anxiety, alienation, and vulnerability we experience living between the fateful tree of Eden and the restorative tree of Revelation."

—Thomas Williams, best-selling author of *The Crown of Eden*

BETWEEN
TWO TREES

OUR TRANSFORMATION
FROM DEATH TO LIFE

SHANE J. WOOD

LEAFWOOD
PUBLISHERS
an imprint of Abilene Christian University Press

BETWEEN TWO TREES
Our Transformation from Death to Life

LEAFWOOD
P U B L I S H E R S
an imprint of Abilene Christian University Press

Published in association with The Gates Group, 1403 Walnut Lane, Louisville, KY 40223.

LIBRARY OF CONGRESS CATALOGING-IN-PUBLICATION DATA
Names: Wood, Shane J., author.
Title: Between two trees : our transformation from death to life / Shane J. Wood.
Description: Abilene, Texas : Leafwood Publishers is an imprint of Abilene
    Christian University Press, [2019] | Includes bibliographical references and index.
Identifiers: LCCN 2018025681 | ISBN 9781684260706 (pbk.)
Subjects: LCSH: Fall of man. | Redemption. | Trees—Religious aspects—Christianity.
Classification: LCC BT710 .W64 2019 | DDC 233/.14—dc23
LC record available at https://lccn.loc.gov/ 2018025681

Cover design by Bruce Gore | Gore Studio, Inc. | Interior text design by Sandy Armstrong, Strong Design

Leafwood Publishers is an imprint of Abilene Christian University Press
ACU Box 29138
Abilene, Texas 79699

1-877-816-4455 | www.leafwoodpublishers.com

21 22 23 24 / 7 6 5 4

CONTENTS

LIFE BETWEEN TWO TREES

*Then the angel showed John the river of the water
of life, shimmering like crystal, traveling out from
the throne of God and the Lamb. On both sides
of the river of life, stretching down the middle of
the city's great street, stood the tree of life . . .*

—Revelation 22:1–2a

The Bible ends where it begins. Sort of.

I mean, it's not as if the previous sixty-five books of the canon accomplish nothing, contribute nothing, and stay in the same location as "in the beginning." No. A significant and lengthy progression is obvious, from Abraham to Moses, to David, to Ezekiel, Daniel, Ezra, Nehemiah, John the Baptist, Judas the betrayer, Peter the denier, and Paul the apostle to the Gentiles. Indeed, a lot has happened between Genesis 1 and Revelation 22—triumph and tragedy, holiness and heartache, discovery and despair, victory and rebellion, good and evil, life and death, creation and chaos. We've covered a lot of ground, both geographically and theologically.

And yet, the Bible ends where it begins. Kind of.

You see, in Revelation 21–22, the seals are already broken, the trumpets already finished, the bowls already emptied, and Satan, the two beasts, and Babylon are already judged, when the voice of God avers: "Come now, the dwelling place of God is now with humanity. He will dwell with them, and they will be his people. God himself will be with them and be their God" (Rev. 21:3).

In this verse, the effects of Genesis 3 evaporate. No more weeping or pain or grief or death—for the "old order of things has passed away" (Rev. 21:4 NIV), and the curse is a distant memory (Rev. 22:3a).

And as abrupt as it is expected, in Revelation 22, we find ourselves, once again, in a garden—peering at the enticing fruit of a tree. A tree unseen since Adam and Eve forfeited their right, and ours, to eat from it; a tree "producing twelve types of fruit each month," whose leaves "are for the healing of the nations" (Rev. 22:2). A tree no longer protected with a cherubim's flaming sword. For here, at the end of the Bible, we once again have access to the same tree we encountered "in the beginning": the tree of life.

And so, the Bible ends where it begins: in a garden paradise, God with humanity, enjoying the shade of the tree of life. The *problem* is: Life isn't lived under Eden's tree of life or beneath the healing leaves of the tree in the new Jerusalem. Life is lived *between* these two trees. And between these two trees, life is hard.

Between these two trees, humanity wrestles with God, embracing and marring his image. Between these two trees, our lives are woven into a tapestry of struggle, loneliness, uncertainty, and hopelessness. Murder is confused with heroism, oppression is labeled peace, gentleness disparaged, restraint mocked, love twisted. The poor are maligned while the rich are adored. The prophets are silenced while the profane are revered. The saints are assailed while the adulterous are esteemed. Kids are a commodity, women are property, and race is justification for abject savagery.

Between these two trees, despair is humanity's native tongue and agony its anthem. Questions abound, yet answers are few: God, where are you? Do you still care? Why can't I see you? Why can't I hear you? Why can't I feel you? Why won't you answer me? Are you even listening? Are you even there?

Societies are immersed in conflict, communities are enticed with compromise, and churches are desperate for a revelation. A revelation bold enough to confront their suffering and rebellion with grace and rebuke. A revelation powerful enough to fortify their faith in times of peril and prosperity. A revelation honest enough to admit that, between these two trees, *life is hard.*

And yet a message bold enough to proclaim that, between these two trees, *there is hope.*

Hope for the faithful. Hope for the prodigal. Hope for those who are mourning; hope for those who are wandering; hope for those who are suffering, running, confused, lonely, in pain, in crisis, impatient, or simply in process. Hope for a new beginning. Hope for a new ending. Hope for a story of transformation that confronts this life between two trees.

THE PLACES WE WILL GO . . .

Rarely does life follow our expectations. Rarely do things turn out as we thought they would. Sometimes for the better, sometimes for the worse, and sometimes just *different.* Rarely does a day go by when the schedule remains intact, when actions done by you or to you are predictable, or when you lay your head on your pillow and think: "Yep, just how I thought it would go." The unpredictable nature of life, however, doesn't have to ignite anxiety or paralyze with fear, for often beauty surfaces in the unexpected. And so does transformation.

Last summer, my family and I traveled to Providence, Rhode Island, to clear space. To clear space to think, to wonder, to dream, to meditate, to pray, to write this book. To clear space for God to move in a unique way, in a way I'm not normally able to receive due to relationships, tasks, one of my multiple jobs, or mowing the stinking grass (which I absolutely loathe). So my family of six left the familiar to drive twenty-four hours over two and a half days to simply clear space.

Clearing space can be such a chore that often I'm more exhausted by the thought than I am by the task at hand when the space is sufficiently clear. So, too often, I don't. I don't clear space. I allow the demands and "emergencies" of life to clutter my space, to dominate my world, to take over my life like oversized furniture in a small apartment that transforms your living room into a dollhouse where you're the displaced figure. Appointments, meetings, urgent requests, pastoral calls, doctor appointments, conflict with friends, the unending array of emails, mundane tasks, and more meetings. There's just no time. No time for rest, healing, playing, or transformation. There's no space. No space to just sit and listen, to be still and reflect. The pace of our world doesn't allow it, and certainly doesn't encourage it. And so typically we don't. We don't *clear space*.

Some of us, however, simply *won't*. We refuse to clear space, because, in a lot of ways, the clutter of our lives protects us from the mirrors lining the walls that expose every angle of our bloated souls. It's easier just not to look. It's easier to find a way to muddy the mirrors, cover them up, or strategically place a newly acquired fixture in front of them to *avoid* the reflection. Clearing space would mean confronting the image in the mirrors, gazing at the disheveled mess staring back—hair in disarray, clothes frumpier than envisioned, dirt and wrinkles fighting for prime real estate on a face worn by time and pain. It's easier to just hide. To dodge the mirrors. To avoid self-reflection. To avoid clearing space.

Clearing space is something that I have to muster up. Something that I have to build up to. Fight for. Drive toward. Something I have to construct with meticulous, laborious precision, like the creator of a mosaic of hand-placed stones that cover the dome of a cathedral. And so, in a coffee shop in Rhode Island, I prayed this prayer:

> Lord, my prayer is that this clearing of space doesn't become the obsession, but the product of an unraveling. An unraveling of the strings of my heart that bind my soul like the giant in *Gulliver's Travels*. I want to break free, and help others do the same. Maybe this book will accomplish little or impact few. Maybe all that I'll find is me created in the image of you, which, I trust will be enough. Regardless, Lord, I'm clearing this space for you. Do what you will.

Finally, I sat down to write. And what came out was totally unexpected. This book is not at all what I thought it was going to be. I intended to write a book on "How to read the book of Revelation," but instead it turned into a book on "How the book of Revelation reads *us*." On how the whole Word of God confronts us, targets us, calls us, and moves us in this world between two trees.

Each writing session, I'd begin with a passage at the top of my screen, close my eyes, clearing space for the Word of God to wash over me, and then begin to type and pray. Confessions flowed and questions arose that began to answer my prayer and uncover the dreaded mirrors of my soul. Exposing *my* wounds and calling me to healing through *his*.

As my fingers typed, my soul whispered the same question over and over that pushed me beyond the book of Revelation and into the depths of the Word of God, passing through James and Jude, Matthew and Romans, Exodus and Isaiah, drawing ever closer to "in the beginning." Passing the cherubim's flaming sword in Genesis 3, I spoke aloud the resounding question, What happened in the garden of Eden? What occurred in the shadow of the tree of life? No, not just the narrative or sequence of events. The question pushed for something still deeper—a question igniting a series of questions aimed at uncovering this broken world caught between two trees: What is sin? What are the wages of sin? What is creation's actual problem this side of the garden? How severe is our sentence? Did we just move from "innocent" to "guilty"? Or was it worse? Something more sinister? More frightening? More dire?

With each new thought, the questions of the Edenic problem produced answers that led to even more questions. Questions not just focused on the obstacle, but the solution: How far does the mystery of God's response to Eden reach? How far does the healing go? Is there a limit to the beauty of God's grace? What role does humanity have in redemption? Why did God become flesh and not just pronounce us innocent from on high? Why did we kill Love when it became flesh? Why the cross? Why the empty tomb? Why the outpouring of the Spirit? And what do we see today in this world caught between two trees when heaven's light shines in the darkness?

Between Two Trees pursues two lines of inquiry (what is the *problem*? and what is the *solution*?) over four separate sections:

- **Section One: The Tree of Death**—What happened in the garden of Eden? (It's worse than we think.)
- **Section Two: The Shadow of the Tree of Death**—What's the impact of the garden of Eden on our world today?
- **Section Three: The Tree between the Trees**—What is God's solution to the garden of Eden that will return us to Revelation's Eden? (It's more precious and pervasive than first thought.)

- **Section Four: The Light of the Tree of Life**—How does God's solution illuminate and navigate life for us between two trees?

The journey will take us to the darkness of racism, the joy of the resurrection, the confusion of sexual identity, the beauty of reconciliation, the pain of our past, and the promise for our present, challenging us with God's voice in the desert, Christ's cries from the cross, and the Spirit's whisper from the tomb, offering to all who have ears to hear and eyes to see a new way forward in this world between two trees.

Through all the twists and turns of each section and line of inquiry, one theme surfaces as a lens through which the divine Word can be approached, understood, and embraced: *transformation.*

THE BLESSED CURSE OF TRANSFORMATION

We all long to be someone different. Every one of us.

Rich or poor, male or female, young or old, *all* of us long to be in a different place or in a different time or in a different world. Even those who brazenly desire to stay themselves subtly long to be a different, dare I say legendary, version—whether it be more patient, more kind, more gentle, more humble; with a brighter smile, smoother skin, higher intellect, whiter teeth, a stronger hairline; a better parent, a better spouse, more well-read, more well-liked, or just *less* like their mother. We all long to be someone different. Every single one of us.

And this is not something to be ashamed of or to bristle against. It's a gift. A divine gift. A gift given in the garden of Eden by God himself. A gift many of us have simply forgotten.

When I became a dad, my children reminded me of this long-lost gift—for every time they asked me to play *anything*, we were always someone different. When I would sit down for "tea time" with my daughter, I was never *Daddy* and she was never *Paige*. No. A transformation had occurred. Adorned with high heels, a multicolored dress, a plastic tiara, and a beautiful smile, my daughter was swept away to the world of Cinderella, Snow White, Elsa, or Belle. With dignity and grace, she poured the "tea" not just as a princess-admirer, but as an *actual* princess in a world hidden from the eyes of the casual onlooker. She sat down transformed.

And, oh my, if I ever made the mistake of calling her *Paige*, I would get a look of correction followed by an exasperated, "*Dad* . . . I'm not Paige! I'm [insert the princess of the day] and you're Captain Hook!" (Always Captain Hook. Never Prince Charming or Peter Pan or Aladdin. Always and forever the villainous Captain Hook. I never understood that. Then again, I was just happy to be near such a sweet princess.)

After my apology, "Sorry, Princess [so-and-so]," we would pick up our cups filled with air and enjoy the best tea our imaginations could conjure. My children reminded me of this gift that as adults we forget: we all long to be someone different. Every one of us.

I mean, transformation is what made childhood so much fun. Growing up, our favorite games were the ones where we got to be someone different. Never once did I say, "I get to be Shane! I don't care what we play—I just want to be *me!*" No, we fought over who got to be Superman or He-Man or the mom or the astronaut or the damsel in distress.

Personally, I always wanted to be Spiderman. Sure, to the outside world, I was still Shane, but in my eyes, the world was transformed into a cosmic epic, a war between good and evil demanding I be more than just a blond-haired, blue-eyed boy. The world *needed* me to be Spiderman. I can honestly remember staring in the bathroom mirror, stretching out my limbs with forearms pointed heavenward and my fingers in the shape of an upside-down "I love you" sign, straining with all my might, truly believing that at any moment webs would shoot from my wrists.

Absurd? Not really. As children, we just knew we were made for something more.

Yet somewhere along the way, we simply forgot. We forgot the gift of transformation. We forgot this longing was a divine call guiding us back to our Creator. We forgot, and now we're convinced that trying to be someone different is childish or even un-Christian. Our culture fights against this longing as well with ridiculous truisms like, "Be true to yourself," "Just follow your heart," "Just accept who you are—without any changes, without any modifications—and reject anybody or any belief that challenges you to be someone different." So we stare into the mirror of our souls, hating who we are, longing to change, longing for transformation, while the world demands: "You can't be different! You were born this way! Just embrace it."

It's no wonder we live in a society drowning in antidepressants and suicide reports. For the one thing we long for most—transformation—we're told is impossible. We're told can't happen. We're told is a myth: You are who you are. Just deal with it.

Yet, the feeling never goes away. The longing never fades; it just changes shape. As we "adult," the desire for transformation may not look like superheroes or fairy tales, but it doesn't disappear with each passing year. It intensifies. And begins to destroy you and everyone around you. For this longing is found in the excitement of adultery. This longing is found in the intensity of greed. This longing is found in the brutality of legalism, the shame of jealousy, and the cries from the stands of the overzealous parents "overcoming" the failures of their past through the athletic exploits of their children. In the binge of the alcoholic, the purge of the bulimic, the syringe of the addict, the appetite of the materialist, the arrogance of the self-righteous, the longing for transformation doesn't simply fade as we age—it just changes shape.

We all long for transformation. No matter how much we deny it or try to ignore it, try to numb it or outrun it, spiritualize it or stubbornly avoid it, the truth is: Between two trees, we all long to be someone different. We all long for things to change. We all long to be transformed. And we never outgrow it.

Yet this longing isn't a demonic curse. It's a gift from God.

LEARNING TO LISTEN

In a world caught between two trees, our souls cry out for a new beginning, but are we listening?

Life between the two trees of Genesis 3 and Revelation 22 can dishearten the courageous, upset the upright, and create indifference in the vigilant. It's filled with demoralizing dissonance and confounding affliction, where questions swell to a torrent threatening to sweep away even the faithful, who desperately cry out: Where is God in all of this chaos? Does he care? Is he not able? Is *this* his plan?

As the tension builds, so does our desire for transformation. Transformation of our family saddled with secrets, transformation of our churches blinded by selfishness, transformation of our society overrun with mass killings, political agendas, and greedy hearts. Transformation of this world caught between two trees cycling ever closer to self-destruction.

Our hearts cry out for transformation, but are we listening? Listening to the voice of God whispering in the wind answers to the mysteries of a new creation. Listening to the voice of God inviting us to view this world and ourselves from a divine perspective. A divine perspective that thins the veil between heaven and earth, that strips away evil's disguise and its claims to sovereignty, that unmasks the deception of Eden and reveals Death's "victory" as a new entry point for union with God in Christ. A divine perspective that recasts conflict, renames suffering, and offers a new tomb that doesn't produce death but leads to life, triumph, and transformation.

You see, the Bible ends where it begins, because Revelation 22 is the conclusion to an unfinished creation. Yes, Eden. But, more importantly, *you*. The new creation Christ longs to complete in *you*. And our transformation begins in a garden with the tree of life—just not the one at the beginning of the Bible, or even the one at the end. But the tree of life in the center of the Bible, the one suspended between heaven and earth and two trees: the cross of Christ. The *true* tree of life.

Indeed, life between two trees is hard. And yet, between the two trees Christ dislodges the fruit of Genesis 3 to move us from betrayal to fidelity, from crucifixion to resurrection, from conflict to conquest. And it is in this collision of contrasts that humanity can live and move and people can have their being. Where both male and female can experience transformation from death to life—*in Christ*.

For in a world caught between two trees, God offers the gift of redemption, the undoing of Eden, the remaking of a garden. He offers a story of transformation. He invites us into a story of conflict and hope, passion and fury, certainty and dismay, heartache and heroes. A story where a raging dragon pursues a damsel in distress with relentless zeal—terrorizing the citizens of a kingdom and hell-bent on devouring them. Yet on the horizon emerges the silhouette of a majestic rider on a white horse who treads with fury straight toward the terrible dragon, disregarding his own safety in order to rescue his bride and restore the bedeviled kingdom to eternal peace.

Oh—and to live happily ever after.

Scripture invites us into a story that calls us and empowers us to transform. To be someone different. To navigate life between two trees by clinging to the tree standing in the middle. The *true* tree of life. The cross of Calvary.

All we need to do is *learn how to listen.*

SECTION ONE

THE TREE OF DEATH

CHAPTER ONE

THE WAGES OF SIN
It's Worse Than Hell

So saying, her rash hand in evil hour
Forth reaching to the fruit, she plucked, she ate:
Earth felt the wound, and nature from her seat
Sighing through all her works gave signs of woe,
That all was lost.[1]

—John Milton, *Paradise Lost*

What happened in the garden of Eden?

In Eden, Adam and Eve lived life between two trees: the tree of life and the tree that led to our death.

Sure, other trees were present, "trees pleasurable to the eye and pleasant for food" (Gen. 2:9a), extending low their branches of fruit as an invitation for humanity to partake, to participate, to ingest. But all eyes were transfixed by the two trees "in the middle of the garden: the tree of life and the tree of the knowledge of good and evil" (Gen. 2:9). And in a move many decry as seditious, unfair, or even evil, God took the man he created "from the dust of the earth" (Gen. 2:7) and placed him in this paradise between two trees to "cultivate the garden and look after it" (Gen. 2:15), but with this important caveat: "[Adam], freely eat from every tree in the garden, except you must not eat from the tree of the knowledge of good and evil. Because when you eat from it you will certainly die" (Gen. 2:16–17).

After parading all of creation before the eyes of Adam in a fruitless search for "a suitable counterpart" (Gen. 2:18), God concluded the procession by ushering Adam into a deep sleep, creating Eve from the dust of Adam (Gen. 2:21–23), and closing this powerful chapter with a picture of harmony and paradisiacal accord: "Both Adam and his wife were naked, and they felt no shame" (Gen. 2:25).

As soon as they eat from the tree of the knowledge of good and evil, Adam and Eve are overcome with shame, realizing "they were naked; so they sewed fig leaves together and made coverings for themselves" (Gen. 3:7 NIV). So they hid. Hid from the God of life. Hid from the God of creation. Hid from the God in whose image they both were lovingly and tenderly created. Why? "I heard your voice in the garden," Adam explains to God, "and I was afraid because I was naked. So I hid myself" (Gen. 3:10). With tears streaming from each word, God asks, "Who told you that you were naked? Oh no . . . did you eat from the tree I commanded you not to eat from?" (Gen. 3:11). Ignoring God's pain, Adam immediately blames "the woman *you* gave me," and Eve follows suit, "The *serpent* deceived me," both responses ignoring God's mourning: "What have you done?" (Gen. 3:12–13).

Acquiring the knowledge of good and evil through rebellion and disobedience transforms God's gift into a hellish curse. Ushered east of Eden, Adam and Eve leave a paradise lived between two trees and venture into the unknown world shrouded with the shadow of the tree of Death.

INVESTIGATING EDEN
What happened in the garden of Eden?

Retelling the account, as above (albeit without the beauty and flair of a John Milton), may convince us we know how paradise was indeed lost. But merely reciting events doesn't mean you *know* what happened in the garden of Eden. For, upon further reflection, even basic questions about Genesis 3 confound the most devout. Like, for example, how does ingesting fruit from a tree constitute a damnable offense? And how does ingesting food transfer knowledge or alter immortality? Still further, who is really at fault in the account? God? Adam? Eve? The serpent? Speaking of the snake, what did the serpent's deception actually accomplish? A mere indiscretion? Why did the action of eating the fruit lead to such a drastic result as purging humanity from Eden? Was God upset because he didn't get his way or was it something more dire?

Even if we aren't all that familiar with the narrative, we're quite familiar with the effects of whatever happened in Eden. We experience them every day, from sore muscles to obstinate migraines to lawn wars with our OCD neighbors to senseless mass shootings at an elementary school. We experience the effects of Genesis 3 more than we can articulate them or define them or answer the question "What happened in the garden of Eden?" Similarly, we struggle with a question even more fundamental to the Genesis account that's ever-present today in our world caught between two trees: What is sin?

We don't take this question seriously enough. Many simply dismiss it as outdated, archaic, mythical, or, equally dangerous, assume an answer woefully short of the true reality. We presume the definition, then condemn what we assume through picket lines, protests, and boycotts of various ilk, but when pushed to define "sin" we stammer, meander, and offer answers that reveal general confusion more than theological depth.

We *know* what it is—just don't make us *say* what it is. Which is odd, given Christianity's core belief that Jesus died on the cross to save us from our *sins*. The astute will respond with some form of the definition that sin is an "indiscretion"—intentional or unintentional—that deserves, nay, *demands* punishment from God. This definition, then, is superimposed on Genesis 3, conjuring summative theological labels and phrases like "total depravity," "original sin," or "original guilt," or even "we are now born sinful" or "we are now born *with* sin." Each offers its own explanation filled with ambiguities that crack when pressed. "What do you mean 'born *with* sin'? Is this 'with' similar to or different from being born *with* car keys?" "What does it mean to be 'sinful' *from* birth? Is sin an action or an inherited disease?" "What time period does 'original' refer to? Adam's? *My* birth?" With each new category, the definition of sin suffocates under layers of assumptions begetting systems, all of which obscure the original question: What is sin?

Our inability to lucidly define sin affects our picture of God, our picture of Satan, our perception of what happened in the garden of Eden. It affects our ability to evangelize, to decipher right from wrong, and even our endurance to persevere in a world caught between two trees. If we can't define sin, everything distorts, for such ambiguity invites us to fill in the gaps of our understanding of the Fall with conjecture that's vulnerable to attacks from the exact enemy we search to define. Without a clear definition of sin, then, we shouldn't be surprised when we struggle to understand even the actions of God to rescue his fallen creation from sin, not just through the cross, but through the incarnation itself.

"But Shane," one retorts, "isn't 'an indiscretion against God' indeed a definition of sin?"

Sure. But here's my question: What if it's worse than that? What if sin is far more sinister than *just* an indiscretion, *just* a violation that sends us to hell? Hell sounds bad, sure. But what if sin is far more terrifying than just a shift in status (e.g., "innocent" to "guilty") or an eviction from a garden?

I contend that this is precisely the case, and Satan is quite pleased with our truncated definition. For if we truly understand the definition of "sin," we'll realize that the result is worse than just hell and demands far more than a rescue mission that sweeps us up to heaven in the sky by and by. Yet to understand "sin" we first need to define another term: "union."

DEFINITION OF "UNION"

Union is awkwardly approached and undervalued in our Western, individualistic societies. Union is a word that conjures up labor disputes or tyrannical dues comparable to a socialist tax for representation you're not even sure you want—that is, until it benefits you to have it. State of the unions deceive, and chants for the "South to rise again" remind us that union, for the West, is laced with resistance. Shoot, even basic community struggles. Each of us remain and reinforce isolation through garage door openers, social media façades, and layers of shame, divorcing ourselves not just from each other but from our own identity, from humanity itself. And thus, union is as elusive as the mythical red light at the local Krispy Kreme. Some suggest they've seen it, even if just in passing, but not you.

In the West, union simply is not treasured, not appreciated, woefully underestimated, and misunderstood. And this is an oversight we suffer from daily in this world between two trees.

Yet humanity is created with an impulse toward union. Toward connection. In fact, connection with others gifts us with our humanity. Babies kept from human touch or interaction develop qualities that are "anomalous" or "subhuman," earning titles such as "weird" or, more ominously, "sociopathic." But through union, humans receive more than presence; they receive their humanity.

A friend of mine used to be a gangbanger before finding Christ. Both his brothers were in gangs, all his friends were in gangs, and being in a gang was just "life." And so was spending time in prison. My friend's brother was in jail for assault with a deadly weapon and, since he was housed with members of rival gangs, he sought safety by starting fights so he could be sent to solitary confinement, isolated from the general prison population.

At one point, he was in "the hole" for four straight weeks, where his only interaction with people was through a slit in the door for food to pass. At the end of his month of seclusion, the guard came in, grabbed his arm to cuff him, and this "hardened criminal" began to weep.

Uncontrollably weep.

Why? He said, "I forgot what it felt like to be touched by another person."

We were made for union. We were made for connection. Why? Because we were created in the image of a triune God.

> And then God said, "Let us make humanity in our image, according to our likeness . . ." And so God created humanity in his image, in the image of God he created them: male and female he created them [in his image]. (Gen. 1:26–27)

The members of the Trinity (God the Father, God the Son, and God the Holy Spirit) are in an eternal state of union. Not just existing with or near, but an interpenetration of three persons in one being—so that what one does, in some sense, all do. Yet the distinction between the three is always retained, because holy union doesn't destroy or suppress persons; it enhances them. Union without obliteration, community without loss of individual identity, individual action without communal divorce.

Created in this image, then, humanity begins with a predisposition toward union, something encouraged and celebrated in Genesis 2. For God brings all of the animals to Adam in search of a suitable companion (Gen. 2:19–20). In the presence of God, Adam names and engages all of the created animals, yet is left wanting, left looking. Looking for a true companion. Looking for a meaningful union.

Free from insecurity and jealousy, God puts Adam to sleep, and from his side, woman is birthed. Created in God's image, like the male, the female is created for connection—predestined for union. The two distinct persons, then, become one—a mystical union far beyond what can be measured or viewed by the physical, although aptly summarized by "they became one flesh" (Gen. 2:24).

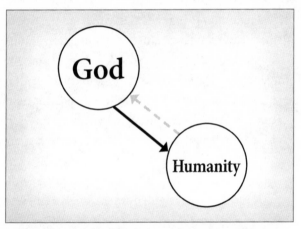

In the beginning, God created us in his image, offering us a capacity and compulsion for union.

Humanity created "in the image of God" presents us at the outset with not just the potential or the capacity for union, but the compulsion for it. We crave it. We seek it. We long for it, search for it, and when we find it we recklessly embrace it, regardless of the consequences. For the "image of God" in us insatiably desires union.

Union: the capacity to give of oneself and receive of another without obliteration.

Union: perpetuating and preserving oneself by giving yourself and receiving another.

Union: two becoming one flesh.

A mystery as profound as the Trinity.

"One Flesh" with Death

When Adam and Eve ate of the fruit, they were not merely disobeying a command, although indeed they were. They were not just committing an indiscretion, although indeed they did. The action was more dire, the result more severe. For sin is willful union with something or someone other than God.

Thus, when humanity ingested the fruit from the tree of death, we didn't just acquire a new status—moving from "innocent" to "guilty," "blameless" to "damned." No. We became something new. Something altogether different. For the skin of the fruit merged with the skin of humanity, offering a union that affects not just location (heaven or hell, garden or wilderness), but our entire being. A union of inversion where, instead of creation, man is now interpenetrated with the tyranny of un-creation.

For in the garden of Eden, all of humanity became one flesh with Death. A reality more frightening than hell itself.

CHAPTER TWO

THE DEPTHS OF UNION
Becoming One Flesh with Death

*Death reigned from the time of Adam to the time of Moses,
even over those who did not sin by breaking a command,
as did Adam, who is a pattern of the one to come.*

—Romans 5:14 NIV

Adam and Eve weren't merely guilty of an indiscretion. For, as Paul himself states, "the wages of sin is death" (Rom. 6:23 NIV). Union with Death. Becoming one with Death. A weaving together of humanity and un-creation with ramifications far more subtle and far more severe than any of us know or want to admit.

You see, union isn't just "holding hands" or "being in agreement with someone." Union is "becoming one flesh," like a bride and a groom merging two lives into one, not just in the act of sex, but through a union with a power and potency so pervasive it ascends beyond human measurement.

Take marriage's inverse: divorce.

A divorce is never clean and neat. Divorces are messy, a severing that assaults more than just a legal document. Divorces leave scars below the surface still sore to the touch decades removed.

Ask children fifteen years after their parents' divorce—they're *still* impacted daily. Just this past Tuesday night, through tears, a twenty-two-year-old student admitted to my wife and me a key source of her pain. "After all these years," she quivered, "my dad still doesn't understand that the divorce hurt us . . . and that it *still* hurts."

When "two become one flesh" (i.e., union), it's not possible simply to tear them apart expecting both sides to be undamaged and essentially the same as they were before the union occurred. No. Whether intentional or unintentional, in a divorce, there's always damage to both parties as well as those around them. Why? The depths of union run far deeper than just the dissolution of a contractual agreement or the return of rings once symbolizing the commitment "till death do us part." Union stretches beyond what the eye can see, reaches beyond what the physical can account for. Union kneads into the spiritual, the metaphysical, the marrow and sinews of the soul, so that a divorce is more like the loss of a limb than losing your keys.

Union is "becoming one flesh," forging a bond impossible to break entirely.

INGESTING MYSTERY

Consider eating. When we ingest food, there's union present between the food and our bodies that is physical, yet still more. The moment the food touches our lips, synapses in the brain ignite as our taste buds assess the pleasure or displeasure of the interaction. Digestion begins and nutrients permeate as the food becomes one with our flesh. As food is consumed, a union occurs between the body and the edible, so much so that to attempt to break this union does significant damage to both. You could throw up the food you ate earlier today, but let's be honest: it wouldn't be the same thing you ate, it certainly wouldn't tempt you to consume it again, and *you* don't exactly come out feeling all that great either. Why? Because the union that took place between you and the food is not easily discarded. After the purge, the food is destroyed, and yet some nutrients from the food (or remnants, however small) are still retained in your body because "the two became one flesh." The food and your body engaged in a union, and neither will be the same again, with or without each other.

This insight into ingestion illuminates the odd practice of prophets *eating* the Word of God. Take, for example, Revelation 10. A mighty angel appears holding a scroll in his hand and instructs John to "Come . . . take and eat" (Rev. 10:9). John ingests the scroll, which tastes sweet like honey in his mouth but sour in his stomach (10:10). John is then told by the mighty angel to "Go . . . and prophesy" (10:11). Prophetically speaking, this narrative sequence is quite familiar, for Ezekiel 2:9–3:4 follows the same format: a command-to-eat-scroll followed by a command-to-go-and-tell.[1] Through the lens of "union," this action (eating) and this result (proclaiming) are not surprising at all. By ingesting the scroll, the message and the messenger become one. The prophet and the prophesy united in one flesh. Each inseparable from the other, so that the messenger becomes the message, enacting its contents.

Similarly, this is why the Lord's Supper suffers when reduced to merely a ritual of *thinking* about Jesus (i.e., "remembering")—for the ingestion of the body and blood of Jesus is a mysterious union where the two become one flesh. A mysterious comm*union* where the messenger and the Word become one, transforming the consumer into that which is consumed. We consume the story of Christ's death and resurrection and then, as the hands and feet of Jesus, as the body of Christ, we become the story itself. The ingestion of Christ's body and blood is more than just a mental exercise; it's more comparable to the mystery of the incarnation itself. An infusing of two into one without obliterating either.

The same mystery is infused in the fruit of Genesis 3. For if eating is union in which something not *just* physical takes place, then unsurprisingly, in Genesis 3, humanity enters into union with Death not just through cognitive assent, but through the ingestion of food:

> When the woman saw that the tree was good for food,
> pleasurable to the eyes, and alluring with its wisdom,
> she took from its fruit and *ate*. She also gave some to her
> husband, who was with her, and he *ate*. (Gen. 3:6)

Thus, humanity's first comm*union*. Or better still, humanity's anti-comm*union*—the antithesis of the Lord's Supper. The latter celebrates union with God through ingesting Christ's body and blood, transformation through the purging of sin, whereas the former consecrates union with Death through ingesting the flesh and fluid of the fruit, incurring the de-formation found in the tyranny of sin. In both comm*unions*, two become one flesh through ingestion, producing a union that reaches beyond location, heaven or hell, and into the very body and soul of humanity.

Adam and Eve's ingestion of the fruit, then, is not merely an infraction of law, but an infusion of Death, a mysterious union with Death. For now we live, move, and have our being inseparable from the path, passions, and presence of our chosen master: Death. Stretching into the depths of hell, union with Death permeates creation as food permeates one's body. Each inseparable from the other. Two now existing as one. Through Eden, humanity is "one flesh" with Death.

And the effects are perilous.

DEATH'S TYRANNY OF GOD'S IMAGE
Union with Death pervades the pores of the human body, invading our conscious and subconscious, leaving no capacity unaffected. Death's parasitic tyranny affects our rationality, social interaction,

intuited passions, governing definitions, and involuntary reactions—an endless intermingling with Death's devotions. Humanity's union with Death is why abandonment is more familiar than community, why retaliation is more natural than forgiveness, why self-harm or isolation or death itself seems less threatening than love. In humanity's wedding to Death, our inclinations center on destruction, violence, and un-creation.

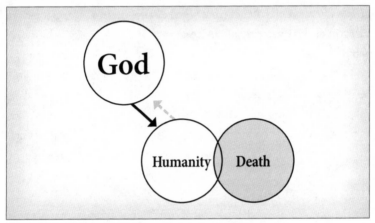

At the Fall, instead of union with God, humanity chose to unite with Death.

Thus, it comes as no surprise that Genesis 3—the Fall of humanity—is immediately followed by Genesis 4—the murder of Abel. This is the fruit of Death's possession of humanity. Cain's actions are the natural outworking of humanity's unholy union, where insecurity encounters intimacy as a threat, exalting self-preservation through murder instead of self-perpetuation through the emptying of oneself on behalf of another (1 John 3:11ff.). Death's comm*union* is not consumed through self-denial ending in liberation, but through selfishness ending in tyranny.

The fruit of Eve's womb (Gen. 4) mirrors the self-centered pursuit of his parents (Gen. 3). As Genesis 3:5 makes clear, the serpent's temptation, seasoned with jealousy, was to seize a gift already promised: "When you eat from [the fruit], your eyes will be opened. And you will be like God." Created in the image of God, intentionally crafted in the Trinity's likeness (Gen. 1:26–27), Adam and Eve exchanged intimacy with God for Death's cruelty, nakedness and vulnerability for fig leaves and shame.

And like father, like Cain.

Keeping the firstfruits for himself, Cain grasped at the Lord's favor, considering it something to be imprisoned, and invited anger, Death's delegate, to feast (Gen. 4:3–5). Reminiscent of God's caution about the fruit of the tree of death (Gen. 2:17), the Lord warned Adam's son, "Sin is crouching at your door; it longs to devour you," to take possession of you, to unite with you, "but you must master it" (Gen. 4:7). Yet Eve's son led mankind further east of Eden, attacking his brother and exchanging life for union not to creation and the Creator, but to un-creation and Death (Gen. 4:8). This fratricide transformed Cain from a beloved son into "a restless wanderer on the earth," now driven from the land of his father (Gen. 4:12–16 NIV).

United with Death, the spiral of violence extends from Cain throughout all of humanity like a king's cursed inheritance. Sheltering us from the presence of God, the shadow of the tree of death ensures Death's indoctrination of Adam's kin. Our union with Death thoroughly penetrates our heart, soul, mind, and strength so that our wombs rebel, our desires divide, and creation resists as our interactions with each other and with God slip into Death's grip.

Death is our warden. Death our end. Death our Eden, for we are one flesh.

Understanding Death through Life
The significance and depth of "What happened in the garden of Eden?" is truly only understood and appreciated by answering

the question "How did God respond to the Fall?"[2] No, not the expulsion from the garden, the calling of Abraham, the Exodus of Moses, the Law or the prophets. Not even the cross and resurrection. Instead, the response of God on the silent night, in the little town of Bethlehem. To elucidate the Fall, to bring greater clarity to "original sin," the incarnation must be our guide.

> Christ Jesus: Who, being in the form of God, did not
> regard equality with God something to be grasped;
> but he emptied himself, taking the form of a slave,
> being made in human likeness. And being found in
> appearance as a man, he humbled himself, becoming
> obedient to death—even death on a cross. (Phil. 2:6–8)

When Genesis 3 is abbreviated to a criminal breaking a divine law, the solution to the indiscretion, the plan of redemption, is also truncated. Whether in practice or in proclamation, many fixate all of God's redemptive plan solely on the last phrase of the above verse: death on a cross. Yet, the first half of this text exalts the incarnation as the essential entry point to the redemption narrative. Not an add-on subservient to Easter, but God's indispensable threshold to restore all that was lost in the garden between two trees, which illuminates not just the path forward but all that came before. For the incarnation of Jesus Christ reveals that the "original sin" is far worse than mere guilt, for when God moved toward us in redemption it was not through a pronouncement of innocence, but he "became flesh." Uniting with humanity by becoming human.

Union, then, stands at the center of the remedy, revealing the original problem in greater clarity: in Christ, divinity united with humanity; in Adam, humanity united with Death. Humanity's union with Death, then, presents a formidable problem if God is still intent on recovering his creation. He could not merely obliterate Death after the Fall, for we had become one flesh with Death. Thus, to destroy Death is, to some degree, to destroy humanity. After the union, the two can't be torn from each other any more than ingested poison can be extracted through a syringe. The permeation is too thorough. The two became one, and therefore, destroying the one, to some extent, destroys the two—a divorce damaging both united parties, offering God only a partial restoration. Annihilating Death would render humanity not "made-whole" but something completely other. A distortion at best. At worst, an unrecognizable mutation of God's good creation. Obliteration was not an option after the Fall. The depths of union are simply too pervasive. Too complete.

DEATH'S WAGES

Genesis 3 doesn't just render us "guilty" of a divine infraction, but describes a union with Death visible today through divorce and ingestion but only truly apprehended through the mystery of the incarnation of God in Christ. Our relationship with Death, then, is not merely one of imprisonment or bondage or possession (although it *is* that), but more comprehensive, more pervasive, more completely transformative on an ontological level, affecting everything: sight, tastes, rationalities, healings, hearts, souls. Everything.

We are fluent in the language of Death, we intuit the movements of Death, and apprehend all reality through the lens of Death, whether ethics, creation, religion, God, politics, family, suffering, allegiances, or even remedies. As "one flesh" with Death, humanity is submerged in darkness, infused with violence, and so thoroughly subsumed with Life's opposite that if Love became flesh, our response would be "natural": kill it.

CHAPTER THREE

DARKNESS FEARING THE LIGHT
The War Within

He was coming into the world: the True Light that illuminates
all humanity. . . . and though the world came into being
through him, the world didn't recognize him. He came to
his own creation, but his own people didn't receive him.

—John 1:9–11

Why run toward Death and darkness? For a wide variety of life's struggles and pain, why do we seek Death's comfort? Why do we charge toward darkness's embrace?

I've wrestled with this question often. Counseling fragile marriages, pastoring confused college students, embracing Socrates's observation that "the unexamined life is not worth living."[1] Time and again this question emerges like a thorn in the flesh, at times discreetly cloaked in other questions like: Why does evil seem more fun than choosing good? Why do we turn toward violence to resolve issues of varying severity? Why do we overeat in times of stress? Why do we cut ourselves in times of despair? Why do we again and again turn to the bottle after a fight with our spouse or a long day's work? Why do we run toward things that hurt us instead of things that heal us?

Why do we run toward Death and darkness?

Every Friday, I begin my college classes with prayer requests. I truly believe that transformational education happens best in community. I want to know what my students are struggling with—what burdens they're carrying—so that, as a community, we can support each other through prayer. Today, three out of the six prayer requests were related to suicide: a high school student recovering from a failed attempt, a family grieving a successful attempt, and another family struggling with an uncle's suicide that ended twenty years of drug abuse with tragedy.

The last one reminded me of my cousin. She's struggled with a heroin addiction for years now. I pray for her often, typically either through cries of desperate pleading or groans of frustration. "What will it take for her to stop turning to the needle as a companion? As her caretaker?" She has three little daughters, a family filled with love and support, and multiple rehab stints, but no help's been enough. She's been homeless, arrested, and even had open-heart surgery because of dirty needles, yet nothing seems to alter her course. Nothing seems to break the bond between her and this darkness.

Why? What will it take? How can she be so deceived? How can she be so blind? How can she continually hurt herself and everyone around her only to seek, once again, Death's caress? To run, once again, toward darkness to soothe her anxious heart?

I get angry with her.

Then I look in the mirror of *my* soul. And my frustration lessens a bit.

I hide from wounds too. Running away from vulnerability deeper into the darkness of my isolation, shunning light and love, healing and repentance in my foolish attempts to escape my pain and pretend it will all just go away. The only difference is I choose socially acceptable drugs: sixty-hour work weeks, hot chocolate ice cream, bouts of agitation and yelling at my kids, or reasonable doses of anti-anxiety medicine. But the cycle is the same and the results are still dire. I run from my past and numb the stress of my present by running toward things that hurt me, expecting them to comfort me. Running toward Death for companionship, yet time and again only receiving abandonment.

Why? Why does darkness appeal more than light? Why does Death's allure entice and Life's embrace repulse? Why do we run passionately, savagely, continually toward Death and darkness?

Or, to state it differently, when Love became flesh, why did we kill it?

STARING BLANKLY INTO THE MIRROR

In Matthew 21, Jesus tells a parable of wicked tenants tending a vineyard owned by a distant landowner. These tenants mistreated servant after servant—beating them, berating them, and driving them away from a land that was not their own. Finally, the landowner sends his only son, presuming that the tenants would respond differently to his authority and status as heir to the land itself. "Surely," he thought, "they will respect my son" (Matt. 21:37 NIV). The tenants, however, killed the son in an attempt to seize his inheritance, to possess the land as their own.

This despicable conclusion prompts Jesus to question the audience of religious leaders: "When the master of the vineyard comes, what will he do to those tenants?" (Matt. 21:40). Without hesitation, the Jewish leaders exclaim, "He will bring those wretches to a wretched end, . . . and he will rent the vineyard to other tenants who will give him his share of the crop at harvest time" (Matt. 21:41 NIV). Jesus says, "Indeed, the kingdom of heaven will be taken from those who refuse to produce its fruit and given to a people who will" (Matt. 21:43).[2]

The following response of the religious leaders is startling. Virtually incomprehensible. They heard how the wicked tenants treated the master's servants, how they seized and murdered the owner's son, and they even proclaimed judgment on the wretched tenants; yet, when faced with the Light, they chose darkness: "When the chief priests and the Pharisees heard Jesus' parables, they knew he was talking about them. So, they began seeking for a way to arrest him" (Matt. 21:45–46). To kill him.

How is this possible? How do we hear the Truth, accept its judgment, and then choose evil? The religious leaders reject repentance and, instead, turn toward Death—entrusting *Death* with their means and their end.

I find that we're no different. We experience Life and Love's invitation, yet shun them for darkness and deception. Like a dog returns to its vomit, we return to our vices, to our violence, to our darkness even when we are caught in the gaze of Grace itself. It's magnetic; gravitational. Yet inconceivable.

In Christ, God became flesh and dwelled among us—Love, Light, and *logos* incarnated—yet humanity's response was to kill? To murder? To destroy it in the most painful and torturous manner possible—death on a cross?

Why? Why run toward Death and darkness instead of embracing the Light?

Darkness Fearing the Light

As a kid, I was afraid of the dark. *Not* the light. I would run away from the darkness *toward* the light, especially coming up from the basement. My goodness, that was frightening. The moment the light switched off, even if by my own hand, dread surged, terror rose, and darkness ensnared. (Should I panic? Why am I freezing? Should I run? I can't move my legs. Did I just hear something? Oh my heart . . .)

Yet no matter the situation or scenario, the intensity of the anxiety or the embellished confusion, light could dispel my fear almost as quickly as the darkness caused it. I remember many nights lying in bed watching the shadows swim on the floor, wondering if my older brother was asleep. Fear swelled, prompting me to pull the covers ever tighter toward my chin, only to find a flicker of solace as I locked eyes with the He-Man nightlight in the corner of the room. A faint illumination, confidently standing at attention with a slight, inaudible whisper: "I am here. Don't be afraid. Trust in me."

In the midst of darkness, however small the light, peace could replace my frenzy. Light could calm my fear of the darkness, providing a path to security and sanity. Yet, strangely, as I got older, an inversion occurred, where in my own heart, and in those around me, light became the enemy. Light became the source of angst, revealing a mystery as old as Eden: *darkness* fears the light.

It's why an essential feature of our smartphones is the password, which some, in the name of personal rights and privacy, don't even share with their spouses. Why? Because darkness *fears* the light. It runs from the light through excuses, deception, silence, or even murder. We hide in darkness. We run toward darkness, trusting it to provide like a mother for her children. From pornography to locked doors to disappearing text messages to hard exteriors fending off any inquiries or interactions, to unforgotten family secrets wreaking havoc on trust and relationships, over and over the world around us repeats the mantra many of us don't want exposed: darkness fears the light. And it will do anything to avoid it.

My sister, Tracy, has an amazing gift of blindness—she simply can't see the evil in people. No matter who she looks at, she only sees good; she only sees the potential of what Christ can do in their life. And she proceeds in conversations and interactions as such.

Tracy's neighbor was an addict. Which drug wasn't always clear, but probably some combination of meth, alcohol, cigs, and heroin. Often when she was shooting up or sleeping off whatever was in her system, her son would wander next door to Tracy's house, usually just looking for some sort of nightlight. One day, Tracy stepped out to grab the mail and saw her neighbor coming down off a high, slumping a bit, strung out on the steps of her front porch.

"You okay?" Tracy asked. "You doing all right?"

Her neighbor slightly shook her head, maybe responding "no" or just scaring away Midwest afternoon flies. Tracy sat down and put her arm around her neighbor and gently asked, "Is there anything I can do for you?"

Tears welled up involuntarily. Her neighbor had gotten good at numbing her humanity, but our true desires have a way of seeping through the cracks in the walls of our self-preservation. "I don't know," she whispered.

After several moments of silence, Tracy's neighbor asked, "What makes you so different? What makes you so different from everyone else I know?"

Without hesitation, Tracy smiled, shrugged a bit, and said, "It's Jesus."

Without warning, her neighbor exploded, "Get the *$@% off my lawn! Don't bring your *#&%@$ judgmental religious $@%& around me! Get the *$@% out of here!"

Quickly, Tracy collected her kids and went back inside afraid. Overwhelmed. Confused.

Tracy sat at the table that night recounting this story to us. "I just sat on the couch, shaking . . . crying . . . asking myself, 'What just happened? What did I say? Did I do something wrong? I was just trying to love on her, and she just freaked out.'"

I turned to my sister, and gently asked an odd question: "Have you ever had someone heartlessly wake you up from a good night's sleep by flipping on the lights?"

She cry-laughed and nodded.

"What do we do?" I continued. "Normally, I cower, groaning some incoherent mixture of 'Noooo . . .' (as in "Turn off the freaking light!") and 'Ahhhhhhhhh. . . .' (as in a "I just flew over the handlebars of my bike onto the asphalt!" type of pain). I pull my blankets over my head, trying to erase the fabric-piercing light flooding the room. Why? The *light* is actually causing me pain. Even if I wanted to, I couldn't open my eyes, at least without things being blurry or it actually hurting, because I've spent the last eight hours or more in darkness. I'm used to darkness now; it's most familiar. So the light only causes me pain. And people are the same way. This is what I think happened to your neighbor: she's used to darkness, not the light of Christ shining in you."

It's easy to forget that darkness fears the light. Whenever their paths cross, a war is present. A battle ignites, often quite suddenly. When people live their lives in darkness, even the slightest presence of light can be painful, causing them to cower, yell, curse, squirm, lash out, and do anything and everything just to get out of the light—to recover the blanket of darkness that offers them false resolution and security. For Tracy's neighbor, the name of Jesus was that light, and its presence offered, to Tracy's surprise, not peace but pain. Through sex, drugs, and abuse, her neighbor had spent so much time in darkness that Christ's name seared her soul, causing an eruption of emotion as she clawed for darkness to cover her once more.

Why? Because darkness fears the light and will do anything to avoid it. The safety and security that light brings is received as a threat, a perilous enemy, a poison that, if ingested, delivers certain demise.

PEARLS OF POISON

Darkness experiences light as torture, not medicine. Take for example Revelation 8:10–11.

> And then, the third angel sounded his trumpet and an enormous star fell from the sky, blazing like a lamp. It fell on a third of the rivers and on the springs of water. The star's name is called Wormwood. A third of the waters became bitter, and many people died from the bitter waters.

Since an angel sounds the trumpet, a star falls from the heavens, and the poisoned water results in countless deaths, many suspect this text (and, indeed, Revelation as a whole) reveals another episode of God's wrathful nature, livid with fallen humanity, seizing them in a murderous rage. The details of the text, however, suggest our interpretation may not be as clear as we surmise.

Three movements of the text must be read in concert. First, the emergence of a luminous star ("blazing like a lamp") named "Wormwood." Second, the twice-emphasized effect of this star on a third of the waters (i.e., they turned "bitter"). And third, the result of these first two movements: the death of "many people."

Movement #1: "Wormwood" is not a throwaway detail in the narrative, but an essential component guiding the flow of thought. Anyone familiar with natural medicine will notice, in fact, that Wormwood is indeed a bitter herb, but also an herb with *medicinal value*. In the ancient world, given the lack of preservatives in food and of consistently accessible clean water, intestinal worms were rampant, causing extreme pain referred to poetically as "wrestling with the beasts" in Hippocrates and elsewhere.[3] Enter Wormwood: "a bitter-tasting herb used as *a cure* for intestinal worms."[4]

Movement #2: The waters in Revelation 8 turned bitter not due to the infusion of poison but because of the permeation of the medicinal, yet bitter, herb Wormwood. In fact, a play on words occurs in the Greek obscured by the English "Wormwood," since the same Greek word appears in quick succession—"the star's name is 'Bitter' [*apsinthos*]. A third of the waters became 'bitter' [*apsinthos*]"—emphasizing the medicinal element inserted in the waters.

Movement #3: "Yet," one objects, "many people died from drinking the water, so clearly it was poisonous and *not* medicinal." True, unless the principle that darkness fears the light is taken into account. For, taking all three movements together, it's not out of the question to suggest that as the light of the Wormwood star approaches from heaven, those accustomed to darkness interact with it through union with Death: where love is distorted into perversion, where forgiveness is greeted with rage, where Jesus is reproached with obscenities, and where medicine is transformed into poison.

In fact, the purpose of the trumpets in Revelation 8:6–9:21, contrary to popular opinion, is not to punish fallen humanity, but to woo them by exposing the union with Death for what it is: a betrayal. In Revelation 9:1–2, when hell is released and approaches its faithful followers, it shrouds the earth in darkness, veiling the sun with smoke, and spews forth hideous creatures to torment fallen humanity, to mutilate and destroy its own (Rev. 9:3–5). Instead of turning to God, the divine healer, fallen humanity reaffirms union with Death, turning to its chosen master for comfort, for protection, for companionship. Yet, true to its form, Death abandons them: "And in those days people will seek death but they will not find it. They will long for death, but death will flee from them" (Rev. 9:6).

In its time of greatest need, fallen humanity's father deserts them, leaving them orphans—bastards betrayed by the one entrusted with their deepest needs. Humanity, however, still clings to Death like a battered wife clutching the hem of her drunken husband's robe. All the while, God woos his beloved, whispering words of life to the lost, crying out through the terrifying trumpets: "Come to me, all you who are weary. I will not leave you. I will not abandon you. I will protect you from darkness with the power of my light."

Yet, incredibly, after six hellish trumpet blasts, humanity responds with a type of Stockholm syndrome, pledging allegiance to Death: "And the rest of humanity who weren't killed by these plagues *still did not repent*"—still did not turn to God, sharing in his warm embrace. "They did not stop worshipping demons." They did not stop worshipping "idols of gold, silver, bronze, stone, and wood that can't see or hear or walk." Idols that can't provide for them, speak words of life to them, hold their hand, guiding them through peaks and valleys of pain and peace. "Nor did [humanity] repent of their murders, their sorcery, their sexual immorality, or their thefts" and turn to God (Rev. 9:20–21).

In short, the trumpets in Revelation 8:6–9:21 expose God's desire and man's choice: God desires union with man (i.e., man's repentance), yet man chooses union with Death. Humanity chooses Death as its companion, receiving God's light as an attack and Wormwood's medicine as a deadly poison.

Death as Life

Some may scoff at such a reading and accuse it of distortion, eisegesis, or worse. Yet the confusion of medicine with poison compels us to grapple with an even greater mystery in the Gospels: Why was humanity unable to recognize Jesus as God in the flesh when he came to earth? And, more troubling, what does such an incredible oversight say about us? What does it say about humanity today? What does it say about our ability to perceive and receive love? What does it say about the effects of our union with Death, since it's not only possible but probable that if "the light of the world" approached those of us wandering in darkness we'd respond with pain and groaning and gnashing of teeth, and eventually destroy the source of light itself—just for a little relief?

And from what? Relief from what? From words like "Love your enemies and pray for those who persecute you" (Matt. 5:44 NIV)? Or utterances like "Father, forgive them, for they don't know what they are doing" (Luke 23:34 NLT)? I mean, how does the face of Grace end up so battered and bruised? How does the giver of life die in such a grotesque and lonely moment, with even his closest friends and family abandoning him to the grave? How does God's presence on this earth end with humanity chanting "Crucify him! Crucify him!" (Luke 23:21)? How is this possible? Or, more intimately, what does Jesus's crucifixion—the execution of the Light of the world—say about *us*?

The incarnation of Christ reveals a God in pursuit of his deceived creation, his beloved image-bearers torn out of his hand in Eden through humanity's choice of union with Death. Jesus reveals a God unveiling evil, traversing space and time, extending his grace on a tree between two trees, refusing Genesis 3 a single victory. Yet, as this love becomes flesh, humanity experiences this grace through the veil of Death, which transforms God's tender approach into pain and suffering, confusion and deception, abandonment and atheism. Fearing the light, we run to the arms of the tyrant Death. Who abandons us. Flees from us, leaves us alone like the Gerasene demoniac consigned to the cemetery and the legions of darkness. Thus:

> He was coming into the world: The True Light that
> illuminates all humanity. . . . and though the world came
> into being through him, the world didn't recognize him.
> He came to his own creation, but his own people didn't
> receive him. (John 1:9–11)

In fact, his own killed him.

Why?

Because we are united with Death—shrouded in darkness and embraced by sin, which shudders in the face of holiness and grace. United with Death, we receive union with God as torturous judgment, a frightening poison. And what we fear, we kill. We malign. We tear down, rip apart, and crucify. For *fear* incites incredible feats of chaos even in the face of peace and truth, and, truly, darkness *fears* the light. You see, darkness understands that while light is its opposite, these opposites are not equal opposites—for if the light continues to shine, darkness must flee without option or opportunity to overpower. So darkness desperately attacks the light, extinguishing its radiance with the greatest weapon in evil's arsenal: death.

When humanity became "one flesh" with Death, our interaction with God, ourselves, and each other produced fruit more comparable to Cain than Christ. Humanity is caught in Death's cycle and so fears what heals, runs toward what destroys, and wars with the image of God in us. For Death pervades us, imprisons us, assails us with its demands, and obscures our senses with its filter and filth. Darkness is now a familiar companion, and Death our native tongue.

SECTION TWO

THE SHADOW OF THE TREE OF DEATH

CHAPTER FOUR

LIFE IN THE SHADOWS
The Grammar of Death

Death has enjoyed a long and checkered history with humanity, whether romanticized or rejected, pursued or adored. Some use the tragedy of death to exaggerate intimacy—as two lovers drink poison to express their devotion—while some fear the presence of Death, avoiding at all cost its frightful mien, from which the most courageous cower. Some court Death as if it were a long-lost friend, expecting an embrace and a kiss on the cheek, only to be betrayed. Others glorify and revere Death, thoroughly surrendering to it and cheapening the gift of life, buying and selling the "bodies and souls of men" alongside jewels, cinnamon, and cedar (Rev. 18:11–13). The interactions with Death vary widely; its presence is impossible to ignore.

Death lurks in the shadows of every car careening down the street, every bird flying in midair, every venture to the cliffs by the ocean, every cry in the hospital's neonatal unit. Death, like eating or sleeping, is common to all. Rich, poor, small, great, all eventually come face-to-face with Death, knowing they are in the presence of a power far greater than greed, sloth, or lust. Death seems to know no limits, as reckless as the sea in high tide. Death scoffs at those who try to outrun it, and caresses those who try to ignore it. At every turn, Death lauds its greatest accomplishment: union with humanity made in the image of God. For ingesting the fruit made us "one flesh" with Death, affecting not just our status (once "innocent" and now "guilty"), but the very grammar we speak.

THE ART OF FLUENCY

"¡Ayúdame! ¡Ayúdame! ¡Un delfín está comiendo mi cabeza!"

After two years of high school Spanish, that's all I remember. That one sentence. And it's not a particularly helpful sentence at that. It doesn't ask directions to the bathroom or a place for food. It doesn't help me find emergency personnel in case of a fire or medical emergency. It doesn't even retain the much celebrated "What's your name?" often central to rudimentary training in any language. No. This single sentence emblazoned in my long-term memory, the remaining vestige of my formal Spanish education, translates into "Help! Help! A dolphin is eating my head!"

The sentence comes from an assignment that challenged us to verbalize a narrative utilizing our available vocabulary, which, at the time, consisted of an inordinate amount of "beach" terminology. This was the opening line to my scene, which I'm sure was absolutely riveting, yet now is a mere relic reminding me that I'm not fluent in Spanish. *At all.*

Fluency in a language is a precarious journey, one not for the faint of heart. It takes discipline, repetition, consuming focus. Complete immersion resulting in complete exhaustion is often the only path forward. Learning a language engages all our faculties: mind, tongue, reason, right brain, left brain. Everything. And many a traveler will attest that over time, these ingredients result in the coveted *fluency*, a treasure hunt guided by signposts of progress, none more encouraging than "the dream."

"The dream" cannot be controlled or manipulated. It cannot be forced or contrived. It descends on the language-learner without warning or expectation. Unlike Mars visiting Ilia in the sacred grove, "the dream" is a welcome guest. "The dream," so the story goes, occurs in the slumber of the persistent language student, where the characters of the subconscious banter about as always, yet *in the language studied*, not in the native tongue of the sleeper. The language desired. The language pursued. "The dream" indicates that fluency is not far from reach, for our mind moves comfortably between one vernacular to another, at least in the recesses of our innermost thoughts.

Death is our native tongue, naturally guiding our thoughts, actions, rationale, and instincts. Truth, life, love, sacrifice, and light, however, are the foreign language. The new language we struggle to acquire. The unfamiliar tongue that, at times, when directly spoken to us is simply incoherent.

LOST IN TRANSLATION

Jesus ignites an exchange in the temple courts, declaring, "I am the light of the world. Whoever follows me will never walk in darkness, but will have the light of life" (John 8:12 NIV). The questions and responses that follow in the next forty-seven verses suggest not just disagreement but a message lost in translation. For example:

> The Jews asked, "Will he kill himself? Is that why he says, 'Where I go, you are not able to go'?"
>
> "You are from below; I am from above," Jesus continued. "You are of this world; I am not of this world. I told you that you would die in your sins, for if you do not believe that I am he, you will die in your sins."
>
> Then they asked him, "Who are you?"

> Jesus replied, "Just what I have been telling you
> from the beginning!" (John 8:22–25)

As the exchange builds, the frustration mounts in direct proportion, for, as John notes, "They didn't understand what he was telling them" (John 8:27). Why? They're speaking different languages: the languages each inherited from their respective father.

Jesus tries to translate—"If you remain true to my teaching, you are really my disciples. You will know the truth, and the truth will set you free" (John 8:31–32)—but the confusion calcifies: "We are Abraham's descendants, and we've never been slaves to anyone. How can you say that we will be set free?" (John 8:33). Invoking their identity as "Abraham's descendants" reveals a logic often overlooked: origin indicates grammar. Your native tongue reveals not just where you were born but the identity of your parents.

> "If you are the children of Abraham," said Jesus, "then
> you would be doing what Abraham did. Instead, now,
> you seek for a way to kill me, a man who has told
> you *the truth* that I heard from God. This isn't what
> Abraham did. You are, however, doing the works of
> your father."
>
> Immediately, the Jews protested, "We are not illegit
> imate children, born of sexual immorality. We have one
> father: God himself." (John 8:39b–41)

Children from the same parent don't always get along (and for some, that hesitant concession is charitable at best), but they typically speak the same language. They normally share a native tongue. Thus, if Jesus speaks truth and the Jews don't understand what's being said, then something is amiss. Something's off. Jesus's response? We don't share the same father, and so we don't speak the same language.

Jesus said to them, "If God were your Father, you would love me, for I came here from God. . . . [Yet] *why is my language not clear to you?* Because you are not able to hear what I say. You belong to your father, the devil, and you long to carry out your father's desires. He was a murderer from the beginning, not standing in the truth, for there is no truth in him. *When he speaks lies, he speaks his native tongue,* for he is a liar and the father of lies. But because I speak truth, you don't believe me!" (John 8:42–45)

Grammar doesn't just dictate what you can speak; it permits what you are able to receive. What you are able to understand. What you are able to hear.

THE GRAMMAR OF DEATH

In the garden of Eden, union with Death didn't just result in an influence by or disposition toward sin, but something more along the lines of a genetic inheritance. For, in this world between two trees, sin isn't only something we gravitate toward; it's the rings of our matrimony, the terms of our covenant, the grammar of Death.

This is why acts termed "sinful" in the Bible often seem more logical or more enticing than its opposite, holiness. United with Death, we crave what's most familiar, what's innate to Death, so that everything pure in Christ is distorted with Death's hue. Lies usurp truth as essential for survival, lust replaces love and becomes common to all, and self-preservation instead of self-denial becomes the zenith of common sense.

Like all languages, pay enough attention and patterns emerge, distinct contours common to all who use the grammar. And Death is no different. In Mark 5, Jesus and the disciples land in the region of the Gerasenes and are greeted by one intimate with Death: a man possessed with legions of demons. The following verses reveal characteristics of the possessed man that correspond to key tenets of Death's grammar.

First, the man is immersed in death. He emerges "from the tombs" to welcome (or accost?) the thirteen visitors (Mark 5:2). Why the tombs? Because "this man *lived* in the tombs" (Mark 5:3). A man disciplined in Death's grammar, unsurprisingly, finds comfort dwelling with death. Surrounded by death. Immersed in death. And it doesn't take long to prove we do the same. Virtually every news segment, Hollywood movie, best-selling novel, or video game assumes death and even, at times, celebrates it. We measure death with body counts (often euphemistically labeled "collateral damage"), average life expectancies, and metaphors like "father time," always imaginatively creating space in our world for Death. More and more Death. Death is so familiar to our surroundings, we often become numb to its existence, not noticing its presence any more than fish notice water. We're just immersed in it. In fact, as I was writing this chapter, a headline appeared on my news feed, buried beneath sponsored ads, sports highlights, and presidential complaints, which read: "11 Mass Shootings This Year . . . And It's Only January 23rd." A headline largely unnoticed. Not discussed. But when you live in the tombs, not much of Death's grammar or presence startles you.

Second, living "in the tombs" importantly implies "living in isolation." Not living in community with those alive, but sharing space with those no longer living. Created in the image of the triune God, humanity suffers in isolation, yet, given our native tongue, is drawn to it, however subtly. Garage door openers abound, text conversations expand, but community is as elusive as the shooting star in a clear night's sky. Isolation dominates through secrecy, shame, pride, achievements, and independence. We wax eloquent in speaking of isolation ("When in the course of human events, it becomes necessary for one people to dissolve the political bands which have connected them with another . . .")[1] and embed it into societal axioms ("Well, if you wanna get anywhere in life, you've gotta pull yourself up by your own bootstraps"). All the while, unbeknownst to the well-meaning and the well-intentioned, the grammar of Death is recited and rehearsed, passed from one generation to the next, masquerading as wisdom and freedom instead of its true identity: isolation in the tombs.

Third, the demon-possessed man could not be controlled or subdued. "No one was able to bind him any longer, not even with a chain. For he had frequently been shackled hand and foot, but he tore the chains to pieces and shattered the irons on his feet. No one was strong enough to control him" (Mark 5:3b–4). This detail puts common narratives in a vulnerable position, for often, at least in the United States, we speak of ideals like "freedom" and "personal rights" with similar images in mind: "free from all constraints," "breaking the chains of oppression," "unfettered, unbound in all that we do," "strong, abhorring weakness, and overcoming whatever obstacles stand in our way." Yet, for the demon-possessed man, this same imagery decidedly pronounces his lunacy, which makes me wonder if our understanding of freedom and its derivatives parallels insanity more than virtue. Typically, whether in word or deed, we define freedom as "doing whatever we want, whenever we want, without any consequences," so long as you simply "follow your heart" or "be true to yourself," smugly vilifying any dissenting voices and naïvely ignoring our fluency in the grammar of Death. As Legion reveals, such unfettered freedom is an isolated prison more akin to a cemetery than to liberty or happiness.

Fourth, the grammar of Death is fluent in violence, whether done to others or to ourselves. "All night and all day among the tombs and in the hills [the demon-possessed man] would shriek and cut himself with stones" (Mark 5:5). Working with college students and being active on social media, I see self-harm on a daily basis. Cutting, eating disorders, self-demeaning comments, overeating, overworking, overwhelming ourselves with "antidotes" for our pain through self-harm. Saturated in Death, we at times go numb and long to just feel *something*, even if it's pain from our own hands—although, typically, we don't have trouble transferring our pain to someone else: "The demons begged Jesus, 'Send us into the pigs; let us go into them.' He gave them permission, and the demons came out [of the man] and went into the pigs. The herd of about two thousand in number rushed down the steep slope into the sea, where they were drowned" (Mark 5:12–13).

In our union with Death, we struggle to hear the language of love, because it comes only through Truth. As "one flesh" with Death, we think like Death, act like Death, and speak the grammar of Death. So humanity pursues unity through obliteration, peace through violence, truth through deception, purity through perversion.

East of Eden, our garden is more comparable to a cemetery: surrounded by death, consigned to isolation, unbridled in our passions, and spiraling in-between actions and thoughts of violence. In a world caught between two trees, it's no wonder humanity desperately searches for peace in the face of Death, anything to assuage the war in our souls—the image of God separated by the grammar of Death. A chasm deepened by Death's greatest weapon: fear.

THE WAR OVER FEAR

The devastation of World War II was unfathomable. The annihilation of six million Jews, fifty million civilians, and another twenty million casualties from disease and famine. Inconceivable carnage. Immeasurable cost. During and after the combat, the world was haunted by a question that even to this day demands an answer: *How could something this horrific and widespread happen?*

In 1945–1946, an international court of law convened in Nuremberg, Germany, to prosecute twenty-two Nazi officials for their roles prior, during, and after the war. But latent in the conversations and testimonies was the troublesome question: *How did this happen?* A particularly chilling testimony came from the prominent political and military figure of the Nazi regime, Hermann Göring. In conversation with Gustave Gilbert, an American psychologist, Göring's headstrong justification for his actions and those of others was challenged when Gilbert countered that he "did not think that the common people are very thankful for leaders who bring them war and destruction."[2] Angered by the "holier-than-thou" accusations from Gilbert and the other world leaders, Göring spit with frustration:

> Why of course the *people* don't want war. Why should
> some poor slob on a farm want to risk his life in a
> war when the best that he can get out of it is to come
> back to his farm in one piece? Naturally, the common
> people don't want war; neither in Russia nor in England
> nor in America, nor for that matter in Germany. That
> is understood.

Desire for war is clearly absurd. Yet this response hardly brings clarity to the inquiry "How did this happen?" If anything, it further confounds. But Göring concludes with frightening transparency—a conclusion to the world's question no one wants to embrace.

> But, after all, it is the *leaders* of the country who
> determine the policy and it is always a simple matter
> to drag the people along, whether it is a democracy or
> a fascist dictatorship or a Parliament or a Communist
> dictatorship. . . . Voice or no voice, the people can
> always be brought to the bidding of the leaders.

That is easy. All you have to do is tell them they are
being attacked and denounce the pacifists for lack of
patriotism and exposing the country to danger. It works
the same way in any country.

How did World War II happen? How did the horrors of Nazi
Germany come to be? *Fear.* The same fear found throughout the
world in every country, in every government, and even in our
own homes.

Fear: a commonly underestimated force, but one possessing
the power to overwhelm the weak and the strong alike. Fear can
cause the sane to become crazed, the peaceful to seize the innocent from the fringes of the crowd, sacrificing them in the name
of societal peace. Fear is potent, imbued with the power of Death
and harnessed in each era to accomplish the agenda of Death.

Seventy years removed from World War II, not much has
changed. Fear saturates our media, proving that it sells better than
sex. Headlines are bathed in fear. Elections are won with fear. Wars
are waged through fear, and violence is enthroned by fear. Fear turns
the gentlest of souls into defenders of atrocities, into perpetrators
of injustices, into champions of war. Fear justifies killing intruders,
bombing the innocent, and killing unarmed black children who
were guilty of nothing more than wearing a hoodie at night.

Fear is Death's lover, and Satan wields it with precision.

It's no wonder the Bible is saturated with the command "Do
not fear." From the mouths of angels,[3] from the lips of prophets,[4]
and in the red letter words of Jesus himself,[5] over and over the
Bible, acknowledging its power, cautions against fear. In fact, the
Bible says *"Do not fear"* three hundred and sixty-five times—one
for each day of the year, I guess.

It's quite odd, then, to read the Proverbs suggesting, "The fear
of the LORD is the beginning of wisdom" (Prov. 1:7 LXX), something

Jesus reiterates in Matthew 10:28, albeit with a bit more dramatic flair: "Do not fear those who kill the body but can't kill the soul. Rather, fear the One who can destroy both soul and body in hell." Commands to "fear God" existing alongside of persistent exhortations to "not fear"? Strange.

I mean, love God? Sure. Pursue God? Okay. But fear God? Something's awry.

The answer is not found in the Law (sorry, legalists), nor in judgment and damnation (sorry, fundamentalists). The answer is found in *worship*.

The Fear of the Lord

At the heart of worship rests astonishment, being awestruck at the power, glory, and limitlessness of the One encountered. One so magnificent you wonder if drawing closer will consume you, rend you, sever you from life itself. One so grand that nothing compares—in the earth, under the earth, in the sea, or under the sea. In this moment, in this divine encounter, the only option is to fall down in worship, trembling with *fear*.

Fear acknowledges a loss of control. Fear pays homage to that which is beyond you—something you cannot harness, something you cannot control, something that deserves nothing short of absolute reverence. Fear identifies the One worthy of worship. Which is why the enemy enlists deceit, violence, chaos, frenzy, isolation, and the presence of Death to elicit fear from humanity. Fearing the enemy exalts him to a position of awe, a position of reverence, a position to receive worship.

My friend Muchengetwa is African, although no one calls him by this name. In fact, very few people even know this *is* his name. To most, he's just Bogni (pronounced Bō-nee). His large frame pales in comparison to his spiritual stature, for he is a giant of the faith.

Late one evening, Bogni received a call from a friend with a strange request. At church that night, a woman who recently converted began shrieking in a voice that didn't seem human. Barely literate, she began crying out in fluent Latin the names of demons, calling on them "to come and join the fight." Bogni's friend asked, "I know your mom used to be a witch doctor or whatever, so do you have any experience with things like this?" With a smile apparent in his deep, bass voice, Bogni responded, "As a matter of fact, I do."

Bogni approached the house where the woman was sitting partially restrained in a chair in the living room. As he opened the door and crossed the threshold, the woman looked toward Bogni with a sinister mixture of both grimace and grin, and with an unnatural, demonic voice, she announced: "So we meet again, Muchengetwa."

Recounting the story, Bogni said, "It was in this moment, Shane, that I was *tempted to fear*. But then I remembered the battle isn't between me and her, but between what's *in* me and what's *in* her."

Tempted to fear. Tempted to cower at the proclamation of his African name. Tempted to approach the demonic with awe, with heightened reverence. Tempted to put the evil one in a position to receive our worship. To receive our fear.

When we choose to fear, Death receives more than just violent, erratic, self-preserving actions from us. It receives something only worthy of God himself: our worship. Yet, as we purge union with Death and draw closer to union with God, we rightly fear the Lord's presence may consume us, that drawing any closer to the Light may extinguish the flame of our life. And yet, as we approach God's throne trembling, we receive a tender touch and a gentle whisper, "Do not fear, my child. With me, you're safe."

THE SHADOW OF THE TREE OF DEATH

In the shadow of the tree of Death, humanity fluently speaks the grammar of Death. A native tongue filled with violence, isolation, infidelity, deceit, self-harm, and fear. Unable to hear truth as true, humanity persists in a world between two trees more comparable to a cemetery than a garden. Humanity wanders east of Eden so infused with the language of Death that *its* reactions become our default, *its* logic saturates our own, *its* presence propels us into a cycle of distortion where truth is engaged as a lie, where remedies are recast as poison, and where saviors are refashioned as oppressive conquerors. We avoid what heals, we run toward what destroys, and we hasten to weapons of division and obliteration. Union with Death purges our vocabulary of hope and love, peace and harmony. Union with Death rewards the actions of racism and unbridled passions, warring against the image of God resiliently present within us—perverting our ability to see God, hear God, or engage him. The results are familiar and blindly repeated by generation after generation disciplined in their native tongue: Death.

CHAPTER FIVE

THE STATE OF OUR UNION
Divided We Fall

I was five years old the first time I heard the N word.

I was standing in the kitchen, playing on a Nerf basketball hoop in light spilling over from the living room. My parents weren't there. My siblings were somewhere else. And I was bouncing back and forth from my Nerf game in the kitchen to the David Copperfield special on the TV in the living room. Without warning or invitation, over the half-wall separating the two rooms lofted the despicable word carried by the voice of my grandma talking to someone on the cordless phone.

My grandma grew up in the South during the '40s, '50s, and '60s, and she carried those experiences and prejudices to Indiana after she married. And now, some forty to fifty years later, she offered racial division to a new generation through a carelessly uttered word.

On my way home that night, I startled my mom from the backseat when I naïvely asked, "Mom, what does [the N word] mean?" not realizing my need for censorship.

She shot a look of surprise toward my dad driving us home, and in the faint light from the dashboard I could see my mom's look transform into frustration or maybe anger.

"Where did you hear that word?" she said sharply.

Still oblivious to the explosives contained in the six letters, I said, "Mamaw said it when she was talking to someone on the phone. What's it mean?"

Not sure where to begin or how to explain to a five-year-old the deplorable nature of such a word, my mom wisely advised, "Son, we will explain it to you more when you get older, but right now you need to know that we *never* say that word. It is a mean, terrible word, and you are *never* to say it. Understood?"

Wide-eyed and a bit stunned, I agreed, and sat curious, wandering how such a funny word could ignite such a sharp reaction.

Older now, I'm more aware. Aware of the history. Aware of the tension. Aware of the blind oppression saturating our counties and churches. Aware of the racism embedded into the fabric of our collective consciousness, whether acknowledged or suppressed. And now that I'm the dad of a black son, I'm a *lot more* aware. Aware of the anger associated with *that* word. The way *that* word overlooks the beauty of the various colors of skin created by our God of diversity. The way *that* word objectifies, subjugates, labels, and dismisses the dreams, callings, and passions of an entire race— including my precious baby boy. If evil could be contained in a word, *that* word would be a prime candidate. It contains the syllables of segregation, the consonants of hatred, the vowels of oppression, the phonemes of racism, and the sounds of a serpent's tongue adept at speaking the grammar of Death. The grammar of violence. The grammar of division.

THE STATE OF OUR UNION

Union with Death actually isn't union at all. It's division. Death can produce nothing else. It knows no other language than cruelty and obliteration, ravaging God's creation of its divine harmony through distortion and deceit. A reality as true today as it was in Eden.

The serpent deceived Adam and Eve—humanity created in the image of God (Gen. 1:26–27)—to consider equality with God something to be grasped, something to be seized, something to be imprisoned and controlled.

> "[If you eat from the tree], you will not certainly die,"
> the serpent said to the woman. "For God knows that
> when you eat [from the fruit], your eyes will be opened.
> And *you will be like God*, knowing good and evil."
> (Gen. 3:4–5 NIV, emphasis added)

To "be like God," though, was God's idea.[1] Not the serpent's. Yet Satan repurposes it for his own end: division.

Division between humanity and creation, as the grounds "produce thorns and thistles," only yielding fruit through humanity's "painful toil" (Gen. 3:17–19). Division between humanity and humanity, as men fight men, women battle women, and hostility instead of harmony conjoins male and female (Gen. 3:16b). Division between humanity and self, as our flesh wages war against us and the beyond, not knowing where the target resides, yet swinging with all the more vigor (Gen. 3:16a). Division between humanity and God—now separated by a cherubim's flaming sword (Gen. 3:24) in a world caught between two trees.

Union with Death is not union at all. It's a distortion of union. You see, union can occur in more than one way, with more than one pairing, with more than one result. Union in the Trinity, for example, occurs through mutual self-denial: where each empties oneself to receive another—benefiting all, enhancing all, exalting all, enjoyed by all. Union with Death, however, is like the union between a parasite and its host: where one selfishly attaches itself to another *only* to receive—benefiting one, crushing the other, exalting the parasite, draining the host. Thus, while it's not inaccurate to describe humanity as "united with Death," this union is infinitely different from union with God.[2]

How so?

"Union" is defined by "who" is involved (i.e., agents) and what the union entails (i.e., activity). So, for example:

"I love my students."
"I love my brothers."
"I love my wife."

Three statements, three unions, all summarized with the same word: "love." The word *love*, however, doesn't retain the same definition in each scenario. We know this intuitively. The expected activity differs significantly in each situation because of the agents involved: student, brother, wife. We not only expect different activities in each, but we recoil at the thought of intermingling them—e.g., the activities between a husband and a wife should not occur between a teacher and a student or between siblings. Because of who they are (i.e., the agents), their union demands certain activities and excludes others.

The same is true with "union with God" and "union with Death." Union with Death is division. Isolation. Severing of community with others, selfishly breaking boundaries and barriers to exalt the self, to benefit self, to serve self. Union with God is harmony. Togetherness. Living in community with others, selflessly reaching across boundaries and barriers to heal others, to benefit others, to serve others.

God is infinitely giving Life, giving himself.

Death is a parasite, unable to sustain itself without the existence of another.

Thus, union with Death transforms humanity into a host for the evil leech, benefiting evil but not the other, enhancing Death but dividing humanity. Discipling humanity in the fruit of division—violent, self-preserving division resulting in un-creation tyrannically ruling God's creation through political disputes, denominational hubris, patriotic fervor, economic disparity, gender inequality, and inexplicable racism.

Even in the church.

DIVIDING A BODY

Division in the body of Christ should be an oxymoron instead of an honored guest. Sunday after Sunday, lines are drawn, enemies are identified, parties cleave, and tension ushers in worship wars and doctrinal debates in passive-aggressive comments from the pulpit and the pews, at times spilling over into potlucks and social media. With one voice we recite the morning's Scripture reading, Jesus's prayer from John 17:21—"may all of them be one [i.e., union], Father, just as you are in me and I am in you [i.e., union]. May they also be in us [i.e., union], so that the world may believe you've sent me"—yet we fill our lives with the grammar of Death and its poisonous fruit: division.

The disciples of Jesus did the same, so I guess we're in good company (although I'm not so sure that's the correct use of the word "good"). In Mark 10:35, James and John, the "sons of thunder," pull Jesus aside and, in hushed tones, of course, they ask: "Teacher, we want you to do for us whatever we ask" (NIV).

That's bold. I mean, if ever a comment set a trap, it would be this one. "Hey, Jesus, I just have a small favor to ask: Will you do whatever I want? Say yes, Jesus! Don't think, just say *yes*! SAY YES!"

Before we throw the stone in our hand, we may want to ask ourselves: Do we do this? Do we come to God with a list of things we want him to rubber stamp, to do without question or hesitation like an enslaved genie compelled to grant our endless wishes? Do we do this? (If you're still wondering, next week just take a look at the prayer request section in the church bulletin and see what you find.)

Jesus, however, wouldn't wander into their snare. In fact, in the previous chapter, Jesus had confronted the same issue. In Mark 9:31, Jesus predicts his death and arrives at Capernaum two verses later. Upon entering the house, Jesus asks the disciples, "What were you arguing about on the road?"

Silence.

They didn't want to respond. Or maybe they didn't know *how* to respond. So they didn't. They remained silent. The truth was worse than spurning the Savior's question with no response at all. Why? Because, on the road, "they were arguing about who was the greatest" (Mark 9:34).

What kind of conversation is that? Especially right after Jesus—whom the disciples had already identified as the Messiah (Mark 8:27–30)—proclaims his own selfless death (Mark 9:31)? Their response is to start fighting about who is the greatest? Their response is division?

> "Teacher," James and John asked, "we want you to do for us whatever we ask."
>
> "And what would that be?" Jesus responds.
>
> They said, "Let one of us sit at your right hand and one at your left in your glory." (Mark 10:35–37)

Translation: "Declare us 'the greatest.'" Over all the other disciples, over all other Jews, over all the wretched Gentiles, declare us, James and John, the greatest in the kingdom of heaven.

This was brazen. Selfish. Reckless. A Judas-like betrayal. Pulling Jesus aside to try to secure the position of "the greatest" when the other ten disciples had left just as much, had sacrificed just as much, had accomplished just as much. This request was very Death-like. James and John grasp at the fruit of Death, dividing the disciples of Christ. "When the ten heard this, they became indignant with James and John" (Mark 10:41). Lines were drawn, and division simmered.

Jesus's response? He challenges their definition of greatness and their addiction to division: "You know that those considered rulers of the Gentiles lord it *over* them, and their 'great ones' exercise authority *over* them" (Mark 10:42). In other words, your definition of greatness and your use of power falls more in line with Gentiles (i.e., non-Jews) than it does with me (i.e., Jesus). For a patriotic Jew who passionately despised Gentiles and their incessant impurities, this comparison was appalling. This parallel horrific. But it was true. The disciples struggled with division. The disciples struggled with dominance. The disciples struggled with racism. Deeply.

EXPOSING THE ROOTS OF RACISM

In Luke 9, after a Samaritan village refused to welcome Jesus "because he was traveling to Jerusalem," James and John sought revenge on the "half-breed Jews." The sons of thunder sought permission from Jesus to "call down fire from heaven to decimate [the Samaritans]" (Luke 9:51–55). The hatred between the Jews and the Samaritans was mutual, at this point stretching back hundreds of years filled with endless accounts of accusations of impurity, declarations of "God's true people," and not a little bloodshed. Sure, James and John merely inherited this racism, but their actions preserved it. Fighting *for* division *instead* of harmony. Fighting *for* segregation (or in this case execution) *instead* of reconciliation. Instead of forgiveness. Instead of repentance. Instead of peace. Opting instead for fire. "But Jesus turned and rebuked them" (Luke 9:55 NIV), announcing a new kingdom, a new goal, a new way forward.

73

Union instead of division, integration instead of separation, grace instead of racism.

Even after the cross, the resurrection, and the outpouring of the Spirit, Peter struggled with racism. He deeply struggled to embrace Gentiles (non-Jews). In Acts 10, Peter receives a vision and a command: a picture of clean and unclean animals intermingled and the voice of God exhorting him to "kill and eat" (Acts 10:13). Naturally, Peter argues with God, "Absolutely not, Lord! I've never eaten anything defiled or unclean" (Acts 10:14). God responds, "Do not consider anything impure that God has made clean" (Acts 10:15). This sequence of vision-command-argument-response happened three times, and Peter still couldn't accept it or understand it. How could he obey a command from God to eat what's unclean when he's busy obeying God's Old Testament commands to refrain from eating what's unclean?

The exchange, though, wasn't really about food laws. It was about division. It was about Peter's racism and Gentile inclusion in the kingdom of heaven. And Peter struggled to embrace it—for even the one with the keys to the kingdom (Matt. 16:19) suffered from union with Death. Even he spoke the grammar of division, the language of racism.

Yet in Christ, there's hope.

The day after Peter's vision, he obeyed the Lord's command, traveled to Caesarea, and entered the home of Cornelius, a Gentile centurion (Acts 10:1). A bit nervous, Peter begins, "You understand clearly that a Jew is forbidden to associate with or even visit a Gentile" (Acts 10:28). Yet humbled by God's grace, Peter continues, "But God has shown me that I should not consider any person impure or unclean. . . . I now realize the truth that God doesn't show favoritism but accepts, in every nation, anyone who fears him and does what is right" (Acts 10:28, 34–35).

Birthed from the womb of Adam, the disciples, just like you and me, experienced union with Death that produces division through arrogance, self-preservation, power struggles, and even, for some, racism. But the gospel of Jesus Christ leaves no room for division of any creed or color.

THE SON OF MAN CAME TO . . .

As "one flesh with Death," humanity is fluent in the grammar of division—excluding no one: "Teacher," James and John request, "we want you to do for us whatever we ask. . . . Let one of us sit at your right hand and one at your left in your glory" (Mark 10:35, 37). A grasp for authority as appalling as the seizure of forbidden fruit. An attempt to acquire glory and power to rule and to oppress friend and foe alike. A reign comparable to "rulers of the Gentiles" (Mark 10:42)—a sovereignty dependent on Death's division.

> "Yet not so with you," Jesus responds. "Instead, whoever desires to become great among you must be your servant, and whoever desires to be first must be slave of all. For even the Son of Man didn't come to be served, but to serve and to give his life as a ransom for many." (Mark 10:43–45)[3]

This response doesn't just challenge the disciples' definition of power, mind you; this challenges their grammar of division. Their self-preserving actions that lead to alienation and subjugation of other disciples, other Jews, and other races. Races God wants to redeem. Races God wants to restore. Races God intended to reach through the promise of Abraham, setting aside the nation of Israel to be a light to the Gentiles—not a light to burn the Gentiles.

The Son of Man's cross reveals a new grammar, a new path forward; indeed, a new kingdom. And his kingdom doesn't aim to acquire more of the same power the world wields and worships.

His kingdom targets true power that comes through a different allegiance and results in a different language. A power more akin to a towel and a basin than a sword and a holocaust. A power that enables you to forgive enemies, not destroy them; to pray for enemies, not persecute them; to serve enemies, not subjugate them. The cross reveals a union that is truly a *union* and not division masquerading as such.[4]

Division has no home in the gospel of Jesus Christ. Division is not the language of the tree of life, whether economic divisions, racial divisions, or divorces of any kind. Division speaks a different grammar than the trinitarian tongue spoken by the Son of Man. Division is the language of the world united with Death. "Not so with you," Jesus demands. "Division does not fuel my kingdom. Betrayal doesn't characterize my people. In my kingdom, racism and sexism have no place. My kingdom's power is different from the world's power. My kingdom's authority is otherworldly. My kingdom's goal extends far beyond the kingdoms of this world and the grammar of Death. For my kingdom is not driven by self-preservation but by self-sacrifice, providing healing through reconciliation."

A Vision beyond Death

I was nervous on this trip to Indiana to visit family. My wife and I had just returned from the Grenadine Islands with our newly adopted son, Robert. Sure, "new baby tours" are generally exciting affairs, but I knew my Mamaw would be at the family gathering and I didn't know how she would respond. Sometime earlier, when we announced we were adopting, the first thing she said to me was, "Oh, tell me it isn't a black baby. Don't do that, Shane; not a black child."

Now, I look in the rearview mirror at my beautiful son sleeping peacefully, shielded from a world immersed in division; a world willing to reject him before it knows him simply because he's black.

Pulling into her driveway, I was anxious, but prepared. Prepared to fight for my son, to protect his dignity, to protect my family from racism. As I entered the room, my Mamaw sat on the couch quiet; occasionally glancing at the bundle in my arms, with everyone else crowding around ooooohing and ahhhhing.

Finally, I sat down next to her. Not offering my son, and not receiving a request to hold him. Every once in a while, she would lean closer, inspecting him without suspecting anyone was noticing her curiosity getting the best of her. After a time, I turned to her and said, "Mamaw, would you like to hold your new grandson?"

The room seemed to stop breathing as my words hung in the air.

To my Mamaw's credit and by the Lord's grace, union with Death lost a little grip on our world that day. For even deep-seated, Southern racism couldn't prevent my Mamaw from nodding her head and whispering, "Yes, I would like to hold him, Shane-daner."

I gently passed my son into my grandma's arms and watched love emerge in a soil that years earlier taught me the N word. The repulsive word now replaced with a tender memory and a beautiful image from Scripture.

With your blood, [Jesus], you ransomed for God persons from every tribe and language and people and nation.
—Revelation 5:9

CHAPTER SIX

SEPARATE WE STAND

*Then I saw another beast, coming out of the earth, and it
had two horns like a lamb. But it spoke like a dragon.*

—Revelation 13:11

Between two trees, the world's economy is sustained by scarcity.
Paucity. The principle and belief that there simply isn't enough for
everyone. A "survival of the fittest" mentality equally excitable
by Black Friday sales or the countdown timers on infomercials
announcing "This Deal Will End! Never to Return! . . . in one
minute twenty-nine seconds, twenty-eight seconds, twenty-
seven—Call Now!" A child is reduced to tears and rage when their
sibling finds one penny and no more to share, like an adult is
reduced to fisticuffs when the last 60-inch TV is sold to the cus-
tomer in front of them who cut in line.

We view the world through the lens of winners and losers.
Second place is the first loser, and participation trophies are
mocked mercilessly: "How dare you envision a world where all
persons win a prize?" The painful reality is that the world functions

on scarcity: there's only so much to go around, so do whatever it takes to get whatever you can.

Airports are brutal. Every turn celebrates scarcity, disparity, forcing the majority of the customers to view the world behind the velvet curtain separating first class from coach. Even the name *coach* suggests these "dregs" of society are punitively traveling with less luxury—a horse-drawn carriage in comparison to the utopian *first class*, a name more comfortable in a caste system than the twenty-first-century United States. The airlines, though, seem to taunt coach travelers at every turn, from first-class lounges with fresh fruit, to express check-in lines, to the smell of cookies filling the cabin, to seats the size of couches, all topped off with the curtain pulled taut by the smiling stewardess whose face mocks your car-seat-sized chair, stale peanuts, and your probably displaced carry-on that had to be checked because there was no room left in the overhead bins because the first-class passengers' luggage spilled over into the coach's carriage with their oversized carry-ons, briefcases, and blazers.

Sorry. I got carried away there. Where was I? Oh yes, scarcity. The principle that announces there isn't enough for everyone.

In 1932, Lionel Robbins defined economics as "the science which studies human behavior as a relationship between ends and scarce means which have alternative uses."[1] Translation? Humanity is caught in a tension: an infinite number of wants and needs ("ends" and "uses"), but a limited number of resources ("scarce means"). The result is a wide variety of behaviors infused with anxiety: Who will *spend* the resources? Whose wants and needs will be satisfied? Whose will not? Who decides? And, quite often, this anxiety isn't agitated through an attempt to acquire something new, but to simply protect something from being lost. Scarcity: there isn't enough to go around. So grab what you can, when you can, regardless of the cost, or you may be too late.

Between two trees, scarcity adorns life with anxiety, which tempts humanity with violence. Self-preservation fueled by distrust. The serpent tempted Adam and Eve with the same principle: God has something you don't, the tree of the knowledge of good and evil (Gen. 3:1–5). And God wants to keep it all for himself. Maybe there's only so much fruit from this tree to go around? So reach out and take it before it's all gone.

Scarcity + anxiety = self-preserving violence

We fight for ourselves to obliterate the competition and seize all we can, because the resources are not limitless and, indeed, quite scarce. In order to gain, others must lose. In order to be heard, others must be silenced. In order to transform the world around you, the present world must burn. Unity through obliteration.

DEATH'S DEFINITION OF PEACE
May 1, 2011

I'd spent the weekend in Colorado Springs, Colorado, teaching a seminar on how to interpret the book of Revelation at a church called Sunnyside. Leaving shortly after the service that morning, I'd spent the next twelve hours or so weaving my way from connection to connection, eventually landing in Springfield, Missouri, around 11:30 or so at night. I don't know if you've been in airports that late or not, but pretty much everything is shut down—the businesses, the kiosks, the gates, most of the lights—which is why I was surprised to see some commotion up ahead. A group of passengers (about fifty or sixty) congregated below a suspended TV, looking back and forth from each other to the screen, murmuring words of excitement. The energy of this group stood in stark contrast to the airport's hibernation. Intrigued, I drew closer, and at the bottom of the screen, I saw the source of the stirring. The caption read: "Osama bin Laden Killed."

I must confess, my initial thought was: "We got 'em . . . we got the sucker." But then my next thought virtually interrupted the first: "And now he's in hell."

I didn't know what to do. I didn't know what to think. I didn't know how to celebrate or join in the excitement, especially since my sermon that morning centered on the conversion of Saul of Tarsus—a terrorist targeting Christians converted to Christ who was transformed into the greatest evangelist in the history of the church.

How do I celebrate this execution? I know what Bin Laden did. The pain he caused, the carnage he orchestrated, the evil he introduced. But I know the story of my own heart too, and I see the same darkness lingering therein. Yet the Lord redeemed me. Transformed me. And I long for the same, whether for my family, my friend, or my enemy.

As I walked to baggage claim, questions erupted in my head with increasing volume: If Christ died for every soul, how can I celebrate this? Am I allowed to mourn the death of my enemy? Am I allowed to lament this death as a loss for the kingdom of Christ? Am I allowed to wish for the conversion of Osama bin Laden instead of his death?

Over the coming months, the questions proved resilient. Day and night, washing over me, refusing simple answers driven by self-preservation. Questions refusing to be dismissed with a response more fit for the grammar of Death than the author of Life. The presence of an enemy demands a response. But there are two ways to eradicate enemies: kill them or convert them. And typically, in our world and in our churches, the former is preferred over the latter. Violently so. Since the grammar of Death is our native tongue, violence seems more logical and more comforting than conversion. To even question my own excitement at Bin Laden's death is viewed by many as treasonous. To ache with pain for his plight is considered unpatriotic and evil. For when we "become one flesh" with Death, justice is *getting even*. Forgiveness is only possible after retaliation or *settling the score*. Transformation is achieved solely through *annihilation*.

In Death, there's simply no other alternative: transformation is attained through annihilation. We "become one" because there's no one willing or able to fight any longer. Thus, union doesn't come through two becoming one, but through obliteration, where only *one* is left standing. But, in Christ, this is not union. This is not transformation. This is a demonic distortion of the world caught between two trees.

THE REIGN OF UN-CREATION

Evil can create nothing. No, not create *out* of nothing; evil can create nothing *at all*. Evil can only distort what is already created. This distinction isn't just an attempt to be pithy and cute, like some exercise in syllogisms linking contradictory phrases to demonstrate a semblance of wit to the delight of a few misguided philosophers or apologists. This is a distinction that, when lost, threatens to consume us—or, at least, any revelation God entrusts to us.

God is Creator of creation; evil is not. Evil refashions, distorts, corrupts, twists, and contorts. But it does *not* create. It disfigures and deceives. Even Death itself is a mere distortion of transformation. When we die, a transformation does occur. We cross a divine threshold—from breathing to an infinite exhale, from this world to another, from life to dust. Yet transformation itself wasn't created when humanity took the fruit. The serpent merely repurposed it. Distorted it. Altered transformation (becoming like God) into de-formation (becoming like Death).

Evil cannot create; evil can only distort what God created and called "good."[2] Evil is dependent on *good* for its grammar, for its existence, for its very definition: evil *is* the absence of good or less-than-good or "*not* good" or un-creation. Revelation 13 makes this point through perversion and parody—that is, perversion of creation and parody of the Trinity.

In Revelation 13:1–3, the beast begotten from the sea crawls onto the banks as a mixture of multiple creatures, a distortion of creation: "The beast I saw looked like a leopard, but its feet were like a bear and its mouth was like a lion" (Rev. 13:2a). Not pure creation, but a perversion of creation. Satan, "the ancient serpent" (Rev. 12:9), bestows on this hybrid beast "his power and his throne and great authority" (Rev. 13:2b NIV). The distinguishing quality of this beast, however, is unveiled in Revelation 13:3, surfacing multiple times thereafter: "One of the heads of the beast seemed to have been mortally wounded, but the fatal blow was healed. The whole world marveled as they followed the beast."[3] Dealt a seemingly mortal wound, the beast from the sea experiences a pseudo-resurrection—a parody of Jesus, a distortion of "the Lamb who was slain before the foundation of the world" (Rev. 13:8). This distorted Christ-figure then wields its authority to bring peace through a sword, unity through tyranny, waging "war against the saints" with one intent: "to conquer them." To destroy followers of Jesus from "every tribe, people, language, and nation" (Rev. 13:7 NIV). Eradicating its enemy not through redemption or conversion but through annihilation. Brandishing sovereignty not through self-denial but through self-preservation.

Evil cannot create, only obscure, parody, deform, disfigure, pervert, deceive, mangle, misconstrue, warp, twist, belie, distort. Like shadows. In the presence of light, shadows mysteriously emerge dancing near their origin with flexibility and poise, yet always, even if by an invisible line, remain connected to their source. Without their host, they simply do not exist. A shadow's existence is married to that which it mimics, yet is not. The object can exist without the shadow, but the shadow cannot exist without the object. So too with evil. Evil is the shadow of the good. Without the good, evil can't exist, but the good *can* exist without the shadow, and, indeed, flourishes.

This is why deception is so effective: it is necessarily a message clothed in thick garbs of truth. Deception doesn't exist *apart* from truth; deception is *dependent* on truth in its form and substance. Without truth, there is no shadow. In Revelation 13, the description and actions of the second beast—this one brought forth from the earth—illustrates this dependency well: "Then I saw another beast, coming out of the earth, and *it had two horns like a lamb. But it spoke like a dragon*" (13:11). Deception is effective because the dragon dresses in sheep's clothing.

Generation after generation, from Adam to the twenty-first century, evil marches forward convincing humanity of different identities and abilities than it truly possesses. Scripture, however, unveils evil as nothing more than a shadow of the true reality in Christ. The Word exposes Death as just a parasite who feeds on its host. And humanity is its target.

Union without Violence

Evil embeds its serpent tongue into our psyche with mantras like "Survive at all costs." But what it won't tell us is that even though we survive, it will cost us everything. Our soul. Our sovereignty. Our life. For union with Death, while truly a transformation, only produces *more* death, distorting the very gift of God himself: creation and transformation into the image of God. Union without annihilation.

It's hard to envision transformation without obliteration. Union without the loss of individual persons. Humanity infused with Death struggles to see union as anything other than the annihilation of the other: the coming together of two entails the destruction of one (or at the very least the complete dominance of the other). But this is a *distortion* of union. A mere shadow.

This past Sunday during the Communion meditation, our minister said, "In our struggles, we can never forget, Jesus was 100 percent human." Immediately, my son muttered under his breath, "And 100 percent God." I smiled approvingly toward my son, a proud father, not just because my son is orthodox, but because he understands that in the incarnation, union between God and humanity didn't obliterate either. In Christ, the two became one without violence done to either—something we simply don't know how to approach.

So, for example, solutions to racial division typically obliterate the other ethnicity either physically or sociologically, the latter through so-called "color blindness" and the former through a lynching tree. Both options strive for unity through obliteration—but a black man doesn't want you to ignore the color of his skin any more than he wants to be hated for it. He wants harmony without obliteration. Union *without* violence.

The same tension is found in our redefinition of the word "tolerance." Today, tolerance means "full, unquestioned acceptance of [fill in the blank]." To be tolerant is to completely accept anything about everyone—complete annihilation of any disagreement or disapproval. The problem is: that's simply not what the word tolerance has *ever* meant.

When I tolerate the sound of my daughter practicing the clarinet, I don't force myself to label it Bach or Beethoven, then pat myself on the back, saying, "Good tolerance, Shane." No, at that point I've either moved closer to acceptance or lunacy. Relabeling something to make it agreeable eradicates the *need* for the word tolerance, which now begs to be replaced with something more along the lines of "acceptance." To be truly tolerant, you *must* still disagree with the other side of the issue. You're simply choosing to *not* act negatively as a result. Thus, true tolerance celebrates union without obliteration—disagreement without violence. Yet what we call tolerance today is nothing of the sort. And so, many reject tolerance altogether in exchange for belligerence, which, ironically, commits the same fallacy as their opponents—opting for union, sure, but only through obliteration. The incarnation, however, reveals true union through at-one-ment *and* separation: 100 percent human *and* 100 percent God. Two coming together as one, yet preserving distinction.

REDEEMING SEPARATION

My God, my God, why have you forsaken me?

—Mark 15:34 NIV

In these words, cried out from the cross, Jesus disrobes evil, unveiling a deep, divine mystery. A mystery woven throughout Scripture, unnoticed by many and unaccepted by the masses: the river of intimacy flows through *separation*.

Like Adam and Eve grasping at the fruit, humanity rages against separation. Humanity reaches desperately toward each attribute of God as if it could be plucked and ingested as our own. Humanity longs to destroy the distance between us and God, to abort boundaries, birthing a union with God by obliterating God. Yet paradoxically, eradicating distinction, crucifying separation, is precisely the path to isolation, to loss of intimacy, to loss of union, to de-formation.

We receive separation or distinction of any kind as an enemy to overcome. Not as a path to intimacy. We confuse separation with rejection, distinction with oppression. How? By misunderstanding the truth that division is a *distortion* of distinction. Not distinction itself. Division is a *disfiguring* of separation. Not separation itself. Division destroys, but separation creates.

In the beginning God created the heavens and the earth through *separation*. On the first day, after saying "Let there be light" and calling it "good," God "*separated* the light from the darkness" (Gen. 1:3–4).[4] Days two and three, however, wouldn't be outdone. God said, "Let there be a vault between the waters to *separate* water from water" (Gen. 1:6), birthing the "sky" (Gen. 1:8), the "seas" (Gen. 1:10), and the "dry ground" (Gen. 1:9) filled with distinct vegetation—"plants bearing seed according to their *kinds* and trees bearing fruit with seed in it according to their *kinds*" (Gen. 1:12). The fourth day includes "lights in the vault of the sky to *separate* the day from the night," distinguishing days, months, years, and "sacred times" (Gen. 1:14)—"times," that is, *set aside* for God. And days five and six witness the Creator filling the waters and the sky with

> . . . every living thing with which the water teems and that moves about in it, according to their *kinds*, and every winged bird according to its *kind*. . . . And God said, "Let the land produce living creatures according to their *kinds*: the livestock, the creatures that move along the ground, and the wild animals, each according to its *kind*." And it was so. God made the wild animals according to their *kinds*, the livestock according to their *kinds*, and all the creatures that move along the ground according to their *kinds*. And God saw that it was good. (Gen. 1:21, 24–25)

God creates through separation. Creation teems with distinction. Life, love, intimacy, and beauty, all begotten in creation through differences.

Still today, a sunset's beauty emerges through contrasts. The vault cascades with an array of color filling the sky with the power to stop a conversation. As the sun fades into slumber, the horizon silhouettes, and a palette of color caresses our gaze, tempting us to believe in the "good" beyond what we can behold. For what we behold is unlike any other, of a different kind altogether. The beauty of this moment, however, is apprehended through contrasts—the preservation of differences. If the horizon looked just like the sunset—indeed, became the sun—the beauty would fade. It would be just two things that are the same. No variation. No uniqueness. Just more of the same.

Separation incites beauty; it invites intimacy. This is the reason vows exist in a wedding ceremony. Vows to be faithful. Vows to be dedicated. Vows to be one. Vows to separate from all others in faithfulness to *this one*, and no other. As my minister, Randy Gariss, once said, "In the gradebook of faithfulness, 97 percent faithful is not an A. It's a failing grade, because faithfulness must be 100 percent or it's not faithfulness at all. It's unfaithfulness." Vows of fidelity, vows of intimacy, are essentially established on the creative power of separation. A power humanity not only struggles with but habitually rejects.

This is precisely why the conversations today around transgenderism and homosexual marriage come as no surprise. Boundaries on any level will eventually be assailed in the name of "love," presuming that unbridled freedom is the only pathway to intimacy. Not separation. Even evolution's "natural selection" becomes an obstacle to obliterate. Nature separates humanity into male and female, but our union with Death confronts these distinctions with violent zeal.

In some sense, then, our world's pursuit of our "true self" has become a subtle yet systematic eradication of "self." But not through self-denial; through self-indulgence (i.e., no boundaries on what I want and can have). We want to choose not only who we "love," but also what gender we want to be, if indeed we want to be a gender at all, opting instead for "asexual" or something completely other. But the Western world is not the first to uncover gender dysphoria or homosexual monogamy—they are present all throughout history, from Sodom to Babylon to Greece to Rome and beyond.[5] These issues simply are not new. And neither is the loneliness or isolation or division that fuels them. Yet we grasp for the same remedy as broken humanity throughout history—eradicate distinctions and separations, believing *this time* such a move will lead to our prized possession: intimacy.

Adam and Eve grasped the fruit to "be like God,"[6] to eradicate separation from God. But, as we've seen, this action didn't produce union at all, but division. Not distinction, but divisive animosity. So how did God respond? By adding *separation* back into the equation. By placing humanity east of Eden, not as a punishment, but as a plan for re-*union* (Gen. 3:22–24).

Separation is God's perpetual tool of creation, or, after the Fall, re-creation—separating us to bring us into union with him. But how do we respond? By raging against separation in all its forms. We construct a tower of Babel to eradicate separation between us and God (Gen. 11:1ff.), but God knows that obliteration of differences doesn't lead to union. So he separates the nations and, through Abraham, *sets aside* Israel from among the nations in order to reach *all* nations, because union is birthed through separation (Gen. 12:1–3). Israel, though, rebels against *separation,* begging God to "appoint for us a king to rule us, like all the other nations have" (1 Sam. 8:5). A request that rejects God as their king and paves the path for regal tyranny rife with division, idolatry, and violence (1 Sam. 8:6–18). After years of despotic rule filled with pagan deities and enough death to satisfy the bloodlust of most, the nation of Israel, in full rebellion against God, is led by the Lord into exile—*separating* them from their homeland, so that union with God is, once again, possible (Jer. 33:6–9). Over and over and over, humanity assails separation while God reinserts it. Why? Because union is birthed not through the obliteration of differences but in the preservation and restoration of them.

THE DEFINITION OF INSANITY

In Revelation 7:9, the description of the great multitude in heaven contains damnation of division and celebration of distinction. This great multitude—"standing before the throne and before the Lamb," dressed in "white robes" of victory and triumph, crying out in a loud, unified voice, "Salvation belongs to our God" (7:9–10)— is composed of "every nation, tribe, people, and language." Union, yet not through obliteration. Reconciliation with God and each other, but not through "color blindness" or annihilation. New creation not preserving racial *division*, but celebrating God's colorful creativity redeemed in Christ. Ethnic distinctions, *separations* that, when given to Christ, produce exquisite union instead of barriers of bigotry. A picture of heaven showing us how to live on earth.

Yet in a world caught between two trees, humanity—disciplined in the grammar of Death—engages separation as a mortal enemy. Humanity perceives distinctions (ethnic or otherwise) as oppressive barriers, ruthless limitations, repressive restrictions that we violently confront in our pursuit of infinite sovereignty, limitless knowledge, and impenetrable self-preserving power. Like Cain, no distinction escapes our murderous quest, for humanity, united with Death, marches on in search of the next separation to devour.

The casualty of this pursuit, however, is not conservative morality (whatever that is anyway) or even biblical authority. The fatal wound is administered to intimacy. Union through eradication produces a deeper loneliness, a more palpable despair, a more pervasive awareness that "all is lost."

This is why when Paul speaks of the church as "one body with many parts," the union doesn't necessitate the eradication of the individual or the obliteration of any party (1 Cor. 12:12–30). In the body, the arm and the leg are separate, but function in concert. However, the entire body suffers if it loses an arm (obliteration) or if a leg decides it doesn't want to be a leg anymore but a liver, and demands to be recognized as such (eradication of separation). In order for the body to be healthy and to function effectively, union must be pursued that celebrates and leverages separation instead of annihilating it. All individuals imbued with unique spiritual gifts serving as "one body," providing unparalleled unity and *intimacy*. "If one part suffers," Paul says, "[if one person is in pain], every part suffers along with it. If one part is honored, every part rejoices along with it" (1 Cor. 12:26). In Christ (and unlike Death), two become one without violence done to either. In Christ, separation produces union without obliteration, "oneness" without eradication, intimacy without limits.

Our pursuit of love through the eradication of boundaries is no different from Israel's request for a king or Adam and Eve's fruit heist. Violence against separation merely results in union with Death—a principle displayed time and again throughout history, whether ancient or modern. Yet we repeat the same steps, ignoring history's pattern, expecting intimacy but finding, once again, despair. If Alcoholics Anonymous is right and insanity is "doing the same thing over, and over again, expecting a different result," then I fear humanity is unknowingly quite deranged. Humanity as one-flesh-with-Death persistently mistakes a remedy for poison. Separation as subjugation. A confusion lamented by Christ on the cross:

> *Father, forgive them, for they don't know what they're doing.*
> —Luke 23:34

EMERGING FROM THE SHADOWS

What happened in Eden was not just a mere indiscretion. A mere infraction. It's far worse. Humanity became one flesh with Death, rending the heart of God and the world's ability to reach him, perceive him, unite with him without divine intervention. The results were damning and the damage pervasive. Humanity's flesh became one flesh with the fruit of Death, producing cycles of brokenness and violence echoing in each heart and civilization in this world caught between two trees. Immersed in darkness, we fear the light, assaulting its presence, crucifying its call, ignoring its truth. United with Death, our native tongue speaks lyrics of isolation, unfettered freedom, and self-harm. We toil in division that wreaks havoc on *all* relationships, divorcing us from ourselves, each other, the earth, and God himself. We are suspended between two trees, unsure of how to return to Eden.

Yet, by God's grace, he separated humanity from the rest of creation by creating us *in his image*. An image that longs to respond to the call of transformation crying out in our flesh. An image that screams through the darkness of Death so its lover can come to its rescue. An image that holds on to hope that between two trees God will startle, dazzle, confound, and create again through means and mystery as fathomless as Genesis 1. An image that beholds and clings to the cross as the true tree of life. The tree of life suspended between the vault of the sky and the dry ground, piercing the horizon like a city on a hill or a sunset in our souls, suggesting that even though the problem of sin was far worse than first thought, the solution may be far more beautiful than ever imagined. For the incarnate God transforms the cross into the true tree of life that shatters the illusion of scarcity with God's limitless grace. To this end, we now turn.

SECTION THREE

THE TREE BETWEEN THE TREES

CHAPTER SEVEN

OUR FATHER REMAINS
Beauty and the Tree of Life

At the ninth hour, Jesus cried out in a loud voice,
"Eloi, Eloi, lema sabachthani?" which means, "My
God, my God, why have you forsaken me?"

—Mark 15:34

When I was six years old, I was molested for the first time.

For the majority of my life, this event lingered ever-present, always near the surface. Yet never something I talked about.

Did I think about it? Daily. If not hourly.

Talk about it? Never. Not once.

Not until the age of thirty-one, and even then it was hard to embrace, to accept, to tell *my* story. The part of *my* life I kept hidden in the darkness of Death, hoping against hope that it would all just go away. But union with Death doesn't dissolve of its own accord. It must be exposed to the light.

So there I was, a father of four, sitting dumbfounded in a counseling session. I'd just finished telling my story for the first time—every fine point in all its gory details. As I exhaled my final words, awkward silence filled the office, only pierced with the sounds of sniffles and a burdened sigh or two.

"Shane," my counselor said, "I am *so* sorry." Shaking his head with tears welling in his eyes, he repeated, "I am *so*, so sorry. What happened to you was terrible. And I am truly sorry that it happened. But I'm so *proud* of you for saying it out loud and entrusting me with this gift—this honor of hearing your story."

He paused, collecting his thoughts, before beginning to pave the way forward toward healing and health. "Shane, most sexual abuse victims . . ."

I immediately cut in, "Wait . . . what?" Confused, I blurted, "I'm not a sexual abuse victim," indicating all trust between us had disintegrated.

He shook his head in affirmation, slightly smiled, and gently asked, "Okay. If someone told you the same story, how would *you* categorize their wound?"

I was speechless.

I'd never thought that category applied to *me*. That was a label for *them*, not *me*. That was a title for *those* other people, but not *me*.

These pronouns are common when someone refuses to face their wounds and the pain that ensnares them, that batters them like waves on the sea mercilessly bullying a small skiff. Denial navigates the angry ocean of our unresolved wounds done *to* us and *by* us. Accusations abound and anchors are severed as we strain at the helm, screaming the same mantra to the unrelenting wind: Will this ever end? Is there any hope? How could my story ever be redeemed? How could this union with Death ever be overcome? God, where are you? Where are you in the storm? Where are you in the darkness? Where are you in the desert? Where are you in this world caught between two trees? God, where in this hell are you?

HIDING IN PLAIN SIGHT

I hate hiding. Even in the game hide-and-seek.

At first, I get excited about finding the best place to hide. Somewhere so brilliant that even when people open the door to the cabinet or walk by the bed and glance in my direction, they can't see me. Camouflaged to perfection.

The person counting begins, and it doesn't take long for obstacles and anxieties to arise. I race to the foolproof hiding spot, only to figure out I miscalculated and *can't fit* ("Darn you, Rocky Road!"). No amount of finagling can get my marshmallow figure into the flawless location, when suddenly the seeker cries, "Ready or not . . . here I come!"

But I'm not! I'm not ready!

I hate hiding. It's too overwhelming. But seeking can be just as frustrating.

Closing my eyes, refusing to cheat—although I can feel my eyelids quivering as if they desire to compromise my integrity without my permission—I finish counting: "48, 49, 50 . . . ready or not, here I come!" Immediately, my stomach drops, not knowing which way to begin. Sure, in each game, you have "hiders" who are just plain terrible—found in a matter of moments because of too much shifting, giggling, or repeating a place from the previous round that was successful for someone else but now has lost all effectiveness. But it's the stubborn few that are fantastic at hiding—covered in layers of secrecy or even in plain sight. And they *really* are annoying. Eventually, against the competitive voice inside me, I cry out, "All right! I give up. Where are you?" attempting to end the miserable game altogether.

I hate hiding. I hate seeking. But not just in the game. In life.

The first game of hide-and-seek was played in Genesis 3. The serpent had already slithered away, and God was walking in the cool of the day in the bounteous garden. The man and his wife, however, were nowhere to be found, since "they hid themselves among the trees of the garden from the face of the Lord God"

(Gen. 3:8). The next verse, I'm certain, should be read with a quiver of deep pain: "The LORD God called to the man, 'Where are you?'" (Gen. 3:9 NIV). Emerging from the flora, Adam answered from behind the safeguard of fig leaves, "I heard your voice in the garden, and I was afraid because I was naked. So *I hid* myself" (Gen. 3:10).

While this account is ancient, the scenario is quite modern. In every generation and all locations, guilt gives way to shame, prompting us to hide. To cover our nakedness. To refuse to be seen clearly, if at all. You see it in the eyes of the adulterous husband, as he shifts his gaze to every location except your eyes. You see it in the abused teen, verbally and physically treated as less than human. He slouches in his seat, peers intently into a world beyond the present, and hardly knows how to respond when spoken to, whether it be cordial, compliment, or complaint. They recoil all the same. *Hiding* in plain sight.

We all see it. We all do it.

And I hate it.

I hate the hide-and-seek games we play every day at work, in our homes, at the store, even in our churches. The happy plastic smiles, more fit for a manikin than a mom of four or a marriage heading for divorce. The all-too-polite "How's it going?" and the all-too-fake "Oh, everything's going great! How are you?" with the all-too-awkward "Good, good... thanks for asking." Our tones and our postures contradict our words. The forced smiles tell stories of brokenness and burdens that devastate every waking moment.

Some can't hide the pain no matter how hard they try; some are just better at it than others. Social media assists greatly. When people seek us, at least in cyberspace, they find us. Covered in fig leaves. We're transformed into a version of ourselves carefully constructed through family photos, mirror selfies, and inspirational quotes plucked or created to carry our crafted image to the world around us. Sure, we know the crying, sighing, and outbursts that went into that family portrait on our profile pic, yet all that's seen by others is joy, ease, and smiles. We know the game, online and in life: what you see is what we *want* you to see. In reality, we're hiding in plain sight.

The sin and pain we carry from actions done to us or by us compel us to *hide*. We hide behind our rights, over our privacy fence, and between two trees, hoping the sun will darken so that no one will see our shameful nakedness. We run to our idols, asking them to "hide us from the face of the one who sits on the throne" (Rev. 6:16 NLT)—clinging to yet another shopping spree to numb the pain, another political candidate to carry out our cause, another rung on the corporate ladder, another task to avoid, food to be eaten, friend to slander, heart to break, or movie to consume. We offer ourselves to our idols as living sacrifices, burnt at the altar of our shame—for no price is too steep when our desire is simply to hide.

On second thought, our "hiding" sounds an awful lot like "seeking."

HELL ON EARTH

I hate seeking. Especially when God seems so intent on hiding.

Sometimes God feels *so* distant. Some call it doubt, others employ the metaphor "desert," but oftentimes I opt for the more emotive "hell on earth." The cavernous distance between God and us. The chasm that feels like a betrayal of promises like "I am with you always—to the very end of the age" (Matt. 28:20 NIV) or a compromise of his name Immanuel, "God with us" (Matt. 1:23).

Sometimes, through no fault of my own (at least as far as I can figure), I don't feel God. I don't sense him, see him, hear him. No matter where I look or what I do, I can't find him. I feel like I wander through every garden and wilderness crying out *his words* from Genesis 3, "Where are you?" but without any response. Without so much as a fig leaf falling in the wind to change the landscape just enough to let me know that a presence is near.

But his divine presence doesn't come.

It's as if the banishment from the garden is more like an abandonment by the One who made the garden. Where my prayers pass through the wind only to come back as an empty echo. No matter what rock I overturn or what cleft I hide in, he's nowhere to be found. Not in the fire, the earthquake, the wind, or the whisper. "God with us" transformed into the God more interested in playing some damn game of hide-and-seek.

The desert is lonely and seems to stretch on for years without end. The Freudian taunt of "creating God as a crutch" rings more true than Jesus's own words: "Ask, and you will receive; seek, and you will find" (Luke 11:9).

But I'm tired of seeking. I'm tired of playing games. I'm tired of toiling in a reality with no revelation, in a society with no conscience, in a world between two trees with no God. "Where are you?" I cry out, only to hear my words merge with Christ's voice from the cross:

"My God, my God, why have you forsaken me?"
(Mark 15:34 NIV)

Why have you abandoned me? Why have you led me to this desert only to leave me alone? Are you asleep? Have you taken a Sabbath with no concern for your creation? If you are seeking me, as you say, and I am seeking you, as I know, then how is abandonment even possible? How is a desert ever present? Where in this hell are you? Why won't you say *something*?

I find that this frustration and desperation are not unique to me. It's both modern and ancient. And for some reason, I find that grotesquely comforting. I find strange solace when I discover questions like mine preserved in the pages of sacred Scripture. "How long, oh Lord?" the psalm of David cries.

> Will you forget me forever? How long will you hide your
> face from me? How long must I wrestle in my soul and
> all day have sorrow in my heart? . . . Behold me and
> answer, LORD my God. Give light to my eyes, or I will
> sleep in death. (Ps. 13:1–3)

I find it comforting that my despair and my struggle are not unique. I don't know, maybe misery really does love company, but I like to think it's different from something as pathetic and selfish as that. Something more along the lines of a cloud of witnesses, a train of wisdom, a path paved by saints who understand better than I that there's power in shouting and singing laments in the desert. Power to thin the veil and see from a divine perspective. Power in offering our wounds and our stories and our vulnerability as an act of faith confident in the light beyond Death's dark pall.

With the psalmist, I declare: I hate hiding. It doesn't work. The personas we craft, the lies we manage, the secrets we keep eventually break the old wineskins, exposing our wounds. When the charade is shattered and the mask unveiled, something deeper is revealed, something stronger, something that desires more than a life lived behind fig leaves. Something that desires to be seen. That desires to be known. That desires to be found.

READY OR NOT . . .

When I was six years old, I was molested for the first time.

To be honest, I didn't know what was going on—in the world around me, in my family, in my own heart. I was oblivious. Innocently unaware.

Before it all happened, I was in the first grade and loving it. I mean, I was finally starting to get this "reading thing" down, the playground couldn't have been more sick, and if you add in all the He-Man action figures and the newly invented "Nintendo," I was, as they say, living life large. I just . . . I just didn't really know what was actually going on. I didn't know my parents were struggling to make ends meet. I didn't know we'd just lost our home to the bank. I didn't know the stress and strain my parents were wrestling with on a daily basis. All I remember is that as soon as we moved into our new apartment in Indiana, my dad's job transferred him back to St. Louis, where he would work all week and then visit us each weekend. At the same time, my mom was working full-time just to make ends meet, just to keep us in our new apartment.

So I was a latchkey kid. You know, the ones who go to school all day, come home alone for a couple of hours, and wait for their parents to get off work around five or six. But since I was only in the first grade, Joe was my babysitter. The one my parents trusted to look after me, the one asked to protect me, the one paid to make sure I was safe. Which is why it was so confusing as a six-year-old when Joe first molested me.

I remember being *so* confused. So incredibly scared. I mean, I would begin the day excited to see my friends and learn new things at school, but sometime after lunch, a knot would form in my stomach, because I didn't want to go home and face Joe.

I didn't know what to do. I didn't know how to break free. I didn't know who to turn to or who to ask for help. All I knew was I hated him. With all that was in my little six-year-old body and heart, I hated Joe. And as time went on, my hate for Joe blossomed into hate for myself and everyone around me.

It consumed me. It imprisoned me.

And for over twenty years I kept my story a secret. I told no one, because what would they think of me? How would they view me? Would they look at me with the same disgust that I look at myself? So I buried it; hid it under layer upon layer of accomplishments, activities, and smiles. I built walls from my pain and entered the room of my own making with the belief that it would protect me. That the walls would keep me safe, shelter me from evil and harm. I hid in this room, locked from the inside, away from everyone and everything. Sure, I knew what laughter sounded like, but only through the muffled tones bleeding through my walls. I knew what friendship felt like, what love smelled like, what hope, joy, and peace sang like, but only through the insulation of my walls. In this room, I thought I was safe. In reality, the enemy owned me. Deceived me. Kept me from life as I cried out day and night, "My God, my God, why have you forsaken me?"

Yet, in this room between two trees, union with Death doesn't end my story because God doesn't end his pursuit. Regardless of my pain or my perception, God isn't repulsed by Death's union; he isn't repelled by the sin done to me or by me. He doesn't turn his back on those afflicted with Death's sting. He doesn't shield his face from my filth or remove his image from my soul. He pursues me. He calls to me. He guides me to the tree between two trees. The *true* tree of life. The cross of Calvary.

THE TREE BETWEEN TWO TREES

Christianity has been accused of being strangely macabre. And rightfully so. Central to our faith is the cross—an ancient form of execution intentionally crafted to prolong death to increase suffering. The victim longs for death, but is unable to acquire it. Both hands and feet are pierced, and both arms are outstretched, as if reaching for Death, feeling abandoned by Life. Central to Christianity is a pierced king, emaciated and naked. Broken and laid bare on a tree suspended between two trees. A mangled mess of human brokenness.

Yet the power of God peaks when the grotesque is transformed into the beautiful.

On the cross, Jesus cries out, "My God, my God, why have you forsaken me?" (Mark 15:34 NIV). For years, I saw this as a rare moment of weakness for Christ. Where anger overcame him and he, like me, lashed out at God under the strain of despair: "Why are you so far from me, my God? Why have you left me in my time of greatest need? Why have you hidden your face? Why have you abandoned me? Forsaken me? Oh my God, where are you?"

Oh yes, I'm familiar with this cry. Familiar with this pain. This loneliness. This silence between two trees.

And with each empty moment, hope morphs into anger.

I don't hide or seek, just wonder and weep. Wonder why God has left me. Wonder why God hides in places I'm unable to reach. Wonder why God has abandoned me on a tree between two trees. In disdain, I cry out in solidarity with the Son *against* the Father, "My God, my God, why have you forsaken me?"

Only now I realize Jesus doesn't share my sentiment; he doesn't share my enmity. On the cross, Jesus shrieks these same words, but from a much different perspective. For while I'm raging, Jesus is singing a song of worship. Humming a psalm of David with an ending and a melody quite different from my own.

The Mystery of David's Psalm

There are 150 psalms. So why, on the cross, was Jesus singing Psalm 22? Why above the 149 others did Christ choose to sing *this* particular psalm? Even outside the Psalms there are other hymns he could've picked: the song of Moses after crossing the Red Sea (Exod. 15:1–18), the song of God's beloved vineyard in Isaiah 5:1–2, or even a prophet's song of lament over fallen Israel (Amos 5:1–2). Over all other options, as he hung on a tree between two trees, why did Jesus choose *this* psalm of David?

My God, my God, why have you forsaken me? Why
are you so far from helping me, from the words of
my groaning? O my God, I cry by day, but you do
not answer. I cry by night, but there's no rest for me.
(Ps. 22:1–2)

Despair. Hopelessness. Frustration that boils over into rare honesty: God, when I need you most, why aren't you near? When the world is crashing down around me, why are you playing some stupid game of hide-and-seek? The psalm begins with a tune of misery, yet quickly shifts keys as David strikes a dissonant chord:

And yet you are enthroned as the Holy One. You are
the praises of Israel. In you our ancestors trusted. They
trusted, and *you delivered them.* To you they cried out,
and they *were saved*; in you they trusted, and they *were
not put to shame.* (Ps. 22:3–5)

Anticipation replaces the psalmist's anger. Hope pierces the singer's disdain. Blossoming from the abyss is trust in what he cannot see, faith in what he cannot understand, belief that God would act once again in a manner consistent with his character revealed in his past.

The pendulum, however, resets in the following verses—the psalmist unable to contain his desperation: "All who see me mock me. Their mouths open wide with insults as they shake their heads, 'Since he trusts in the LORD, let the LORD rescue him . . . if he delights in him so'" (Ps. 22:7–8). Acknowledging God's faithful provision from birth (Ps. 22:9–10), the hymn erupts in a fervent plea, "Do not be far from me [oh God], for trouble is near and there's no one to help" (Ps. 22:11). From one extreme to the next, David wrestles with the blinding darkness between two trees that obscures healing, hope, and God. His anguish, though, climaxes with imagery more fit for a crucifixion than halls of worship:

> Dogs surround me, a gang of evildoers encircle me.
> *They pierce my hands and my feet.* I can count all my
> bones. People stare and gloat over me. *They divide*
> *my clothes among them and cast lots for my garment.*
> (Ps. 22:16–18)

Maybe this is why Jesus was singing this psalm. The narrative parallels his own. And strikingly so.

Yet there seems to be more. More to this hymn than just history in advance. More to this psalm than just a depiction of Christ's pain. Indeed, as the melody unfolds, this hymn that began with despair cantillates a chorus of victory piercing all darkness. It sings a song that reveals a mystery obscured by the fig leaves employed to keep us from the face of God. A mystery now proclaimed in the face of Christ: the Father never abandons his children, never turns his face from his own, never forsakes them or leaves them alone in the darkness between two trees.

> You who fear the LORD: praise him! All the offspring
> of Jacob: glorify him! Stand in awe before him, all the
> offspring of Israel! *For he did not despise or scorn the*
> *suffering of the afflicted one; he did not hide his face from*
> *him but has heard his cry for help.* (Ps. 22:23–24)

HE HAS DONE IT

It's easy to mistake Christ's song of worship as an indictment against the Father: "My God, my God, why have you forsaken me?" But Jesus chose this psalm of David deliberately to unveil the opposite: God *never* leaves us even in our union with Death. In our lives, as in the cross, what seems like desertion is actually deliverance; what seems like abandonment is actually intimacy; what seems like a desert is actually a divine oasis brimming with living water.

Scripture reveals the same message time and again. It's in the desert where God works his greatest miracles of protection, proclamation, revelation, and victory. Moses received the name of the great "I Am" *in the desert* (Exod. 3:1ff.); the nation of Israel marched as the Red Sea parted for their Exodus *into the desert* (Exod. 15:22ff.); God gives the grace of the law *in the desert* (Exod. 20:1ff.); John the Baptist proclaims the coming kingdom of God *in the desert* (Matt. 3:1–3); Christ treads on the serpent's head, spurning each of Satan's temptations *in the desert* (Matt. 4:1–11). And it's *in the desert* of our own stories, of our own pain, where we can find an intimacy with God that far surpasses what's present in the plushness of a meadow. For *in the desert* there's no sustenance but him, no bread but him. There's no food for the feast, so we must feast *on him*—his body and his blood.

And as the scales fall from our eyes, we're able to see the beauty of a God hiding in plain sight. We're able to see the glory of a God who seeks us in the void between two trees. We're able to see the tenderness of a God who never abandons his children in their time of need. He never turns his back on his children toiling with the grammar of Death. He never neglects the abused; never ignores the afflicted; never hides his face from those seeking him, seeking Eden in a world wed with Death. We're able to see the power of God peak as it transforms the grotesque into the beautiful.

And then, we're able to sing.

To sing in unison with Christ the same melody from Psalm 22, knowing that its beginning is far different from its end. Yes, the song opens on a chord of disdain, but it concludes on a chorus of triumph:

All the rich of the earth will feast and bow down in worship. All who go down to the dust will fall down before him—those who can't keep themselves alive. Posterity will serve him; future generations will be told about the Lord. They will come and they will proclaim his righteous deeds to a people yet unborn, announcing: *He has done it!* (Ps. 22:29–31)

Which raises the question: *What exactly* has he done?

CHAPTER EIGHT

"It Is Finished"
Embracing Death to Find Life

Going a little farther, [Jesus] fell on his face in prayer,
crying out, "My Father, if it is possible, let this cup
pass from me. Yet not as I will, but as you will."

—Matthew 26:39

On the night of his betrayal, Jesus fell to his knees in a garden. No, not Eden or anything like it. This garden was more akin to a tomb. This garden was shrouded in darkness instead of the light and vitality of Genesis 1. This garden was immersed in doubt instead of the promise and anticipation of Genesis 2. This garden, of Gethsemane, cultivated separation, crops of isolation, harvests of abandonment, and the poisonous fruit of temptation. Gethsemane blossomed east of Eden, in a world caught between two trees, with the promise of another tree still to come whose fruit swells with pain and suffering. In this garden, Jesus fell to his knees as loneliness lurked, longing to devour and derail all of humanity, including the Son of Man.

Between two trees, life is lonely. The veil between heaven and earth can appear impermeable: prayers do not penetrate, worship does not permeate, and questions go unanswered. Especially in a context of conflict, the distance between heaven and earth can feel cavernous. Even in the middle of a garden, even from the mouth of the incarnate Christ, separation can be so consuming, alienation so disquieting that the only request proposed is: please, don't leave me alone (Matt. 26:38).

As the "large crowd" approached Gethsemane (Matt. 26:47b), Jesus was alone. Judas's betrayal (26:46–47), Peter's ignorance (26:51–52, 69–74), the disciples' dereliction (26:56b), the Sanhedrin's contrived conviction (26:57–68), Pilate's self-preservation (27:11–26), and the unbridled violence of the Roman soldiers (27:27–31) each, in their own way and with their own gravity, confirmed the daunting truth: Jesus was alone. Even his companions on the cross—the two insurrectionists crucified on his right and on his left—distanced themselves from Jesus by hurling insults into the air (27:44) to match the mocking of the chief priests, the scribes, the elders (27:41), and those just passing by (27:39).[1] Between two trees, Jesus was alone. In Gethsemane, Christ was immersed in loneliness evident in his pleas to his disciples, "Stay here with me; stay awake with me" (Matt. 26:38b). Whoever is left, whoever is awake, just stay with me. Please don't leave me alone; just stay near.

Humanity is familiar with this plea, with this plight. In the face of conflict (whether seen or unseen), in our union with Death, we, like Christ, cry out, "My soul is overwhelmed with grief—as if I were dying" (Matt. 26:38a). We cry out in desperation, "Father, please, if there's any other way, take this cup from me" (26:39b).[2] We cry out in fragile hope, "But may your will be done" (26:42b).

We cry out longing for relief, longing for courage, longing for the cup of death to pass. We cry out longing for community—even if only for an hour (Matt. 26:40). We cry out for intimacy. Divine intimacy. *True* union.

But God responds, "There is no other way. Drink the cup. Take up your cross. The time has come."

THE INCARNATION OF THE CROSS

Each Gospel ends at the cross. Details vary and different points are emphasized, but Matthew, Mark, Luke, and John each end their story of redemption with Jesus suspended between heaven and earth on a tree between two trees. But what did the cross of Christ accomplish? What role does it play in humanity's redemption? Or, to state it differently, "What is finished?"

John's account of the cross, like the other Gospels, ends with a "loud cry," with Jesus screaming before his final breath. Yet unlike the other Gospels, John records the pierced king's last words with this declaration: "It is finished" (John 19:30). In John's Gospel alone, the crucified Christ proclaims: "It is over. It has been completed. It has been accomplished. It has come to an end. *It is finished.*"

But what is finished? What has been completed? What has come to an end?

His life? Well, that's true, but most intuit something more, something a bit less anticlimactic. Many opt for the answer "payment for sin." What is finished is sin's outstanding debt. To be sure, this answer *must be* included in whatever option we herald. Scripture attests time and again to Christ's atoning sacrifice on the cross:

> 1 Corinthians 15:3–"Christ died for our sins according to the Scriptures . . ." (NIV).
>
> Galatians 3:13–"Christ ransomed us from the curse of the law by becoming a curse on behalf of us, for it is written: 'Cursed is everyone who is hung on a tree.'"
>
> Hebrews 9:15–"Christ is the mediator of a new covenant . . . now that he has died to set them free from the sins committed under the first covenant" (NIV).

Mark 10:45-"[The Son of Man came] to give his life as a ransom for many" (NIV).

What is finished? The wages of sin.

But the wages sin demanded wasn't a transaction alone. While the solution includes this reality, the remedy must match the severity of the problem. As we've already seen, the problem of Genesis 3 wasn't only an infraction of the law. It was far worse. Humanity became "one flesh" with Death.[3]

The "wages" of sin (or the "essential end of sin" or the "necessary conclusion of sin") *is*, indeed, Death, because sin is *union with Death*. Sin isn't *just* a debt for which death is the consequence. Sin is willful union with Death, ingestion of Death, de-formation. And thus, Christ's cross can't *only* be transferring humanity from the status of "guilty of a damnable offense" to "innocent of all charges." Sin is un-creation, becoming "one flesh" with Death, which limits our capacity to unite with others, with God, and even with ourselves (humanity created in the image of God now marred with Death's sting). Thus, since the problem of Eden is far more pervasive than first thought, so too must be the solution.[4]

COUNTING TO SEVEN

So, what "is finished" on the cross? To answer this question we need to learn how *to count*.

After Jesus turns water into wine at a family wedding, John remarks, "What Jesus did here in Cana of Galilee was the first of the signs through which he revealed his glory" (John 2:11 NIV). With the word "first," John invites the reader *to count*, for if there's a "first," we can presume there's at least a "second."

Two chapters later, Jesus is approached by "a royal official whose son was sick in Capernaum" (John 4:46b). Casting aside all dignity, the royal official "begged [Jesus] to come down and heal his son, for he was close to death" (John 4:47).[5] Without visiting the child, seeing the child, or knowing the child, Jesus commands, "Go, your son will live" (John 4:50). As the man journeyed home, his servants intercepted him on the road "announcing that his boy was alive and well" (John 4:51)—his boy had been healed at "the exact time Jesus said to him, 'Your son will live'" (John 4:53). John concludes this miraculous event reminding us *to count*: "This was the second sign Jesus performed" (John 4:54 NIV).

So, with the prompts in place, *count* we shall. The third sign is in John 5:1–15, where Jesus heals the lame man by the pool of Bethesda on the Sabbath. The fourth sign is in the very next chapter (John 6:1–15) when Jesus feeds the five thousand with seven pieces of food (five loaves and two fish). The fifth sign is in John 9:1–34 where Jesus heals the man who was born blind, which is followed by the sixth sign in John 11:1–44, where Jesus resurrects Lazarus from the dead, bringing life from the tomb, man from the earth.

The seventh sign, though, doesn't appear in chapter 12 where Jesus triumphantly enters Jerusalem or in chapter 13 where Jesus washes his disciples' feet at the Last Supper. In fact, the seventh sign doesn't occur in chapters 14, 15, 16, 17, or 18. No, the seventh sign of John comes in chapter 19, where Jesus is mocked, beaten, and adorned with a crown of thorns as the crowd and Jewish officials melodically chant, "Crucify him! Crucify him!" (John 19:1–6). The seventh sign of John's Gospel is the cross—where Jesus cries out with his final breath: "*It is finished*" (John 19:30). A moment of heart-stopping significance, especially if you know how *to count*.

In Jewish numerology, often employed in Jewish literature, seven is a number of "completion." A number of completion usually attached *to creation*. Why? Because God created the heavens and the earth in seven days. Seven is the number of days in which God completed his creation, ending the sixth day with a smile and a Sabbath to follow. In seven days, creation was completed. In seven days, *it was finished.*

Creation allusions in John's Gospel, however, are not merely embedded in numerology. John begins his Gospel, in fact, with a summary of Genesis 1–3—creation and union with Death. John 1:1–3 evokes Genesis 1:1 and abridges the seven days of creation centered on the divine presence of "The Word":

> *In the beginning* was the Word. The Word was with God, and the Word was God. The Word was with God *in the beginning*. Through [the Word] all things were made; without him nothing was made that has been made.

In Genesis, the birth of the cosmos peaks on the sixth day with the creation of male and female in the image of God (1:26–27), and John follows suit: "In him was life, and the life was the light of all humanity" (John 1:4). Christian or non-Christian, male or female, all humanity was created in the image of God, with the light of God, a gift marred by the Fall yet never dissolved, for "the darkness has not overcome it" (John 1:5 NIV). Union with Death in Genesis 3, though, deceives humanity, distorts our vision so that when "the True Light that illuminates all humanity . . . was in the world, and though the world came into being through him, the world didn't recognize him" (John 1:9–10). The world failed to see their own image reflected in his very person, for "he came to his own creation, but his own people didn't receive him" (John 1:11).

John then brings "the beginning" full circle with the entry point to redemption, the key to answering the question "What *is finished* on the cross?": "The Word became flesh and made his dwelling among us" (John 1:14 NIV). The Word, which in the beginning created all things, *became flesh* to redeem all things. The beginning of John's Gospel, therefore, reminds us of a truth commonly overlooked: the mystery of redemption embedded in the seventh sign, contained in the cross of Christ, doesn't begin at Good Friday or Easter morning. It begins at Christmas. At Jesus's birth. At the ineffable mystery of his incarnation where God became flesh.

LIFE'S DESCENT INTO DEATH

Genesis 3 and its effects exploit at least two significant obstacles that must be addressed in order for God to redeem creation. First, God does not have direct access to Death. The concept is simple, but the consequence substantial: the Infinite is not finite, the Immortal is not mortal, Life is not Death. Eden reveals that Death is a refusal of Life. A rejection of connection with Life, with God himself. But God doesn't have the option to refuse himself and still be God. God is eternally faithful; God is life itself. Thus, God cannot die as God. He doesn't have the option. God has no access to Death.

Second, as mentioned before, God can't just obliterate Death without damaging (or destroying) humanity as well.[6] Death hides too, covering itself with fig leaves. Death cowers in the shadow of Adam and Eve's sin, hiding behind its union with humanity, shielding itself with creation to prevent God from swallowing Death whole. Humanity's union with Death means the obliteration of Death would destroy humanity as well. God, however, will not allow Genesis 3 a single victory. Not one. So a different solution beyond the violence of obliteration must be pursued.

Both obstacles are formidable and, to some extent, appear insurmountable. Yet to redeem humanity, both obstacles must be overcome. God's solution, "the mystery hidden from the ages and from the generations" (Col. 1:26), is *the incarnation*. The birth of Jesus—Immanuel, "God with us" (Matt. 1:23). The incarnation of Christ where God became human, where the Incorruptible became corruptible, the Immortal became mortal, the Word became flesh.

To redeem humanity united with Death, God gained access to Death by becoming human. As Paul writes in Philippians 2:6–8:

> Christ Jesus: Who, being in the form of God, did not
> regard equality with God something to be grasped;
> but he emptied himself, taking the form of a slave,
> being made in human likeness. And being found in
> appearance as a man, he humbled himself, becoming
> obedient to death—even death on a cross.

To redeem humanity, God didn't obliterate Death, but honored humanity's choice, honored humanity's union with Death, by becoming flesh *and* embracing the wages of sin: death itself.

Yet mere union with Death is not enough. God's redemptive act must be union with Death *through faithfulness*, or as Philippians 2 states, through "obedience"—not, as with Adam, through rebellion or sin. Thus, the union with Death at Christ's tree doesn't replicate Eden, but redeems it. In Eden, humanity was deceived into disobedience. We became one with Death through *deception*, believing Death was a person to embrace. But this union was a fraud, a façade, an elaborate betrayal marring the image of God in us with the stains of the serpent's fruit. In reality, union with Death was no union at all. It was division. Fragmentation. A distortion.[7]

In Gethsemane, Christ chose death through obedience. Not disobedience. Not deception. Christ's union with death was birthed through fidelity and divine clarity; not through rebellion but through faithfulness; not through sin but through holiness, righteousness, purity. Christ was not deceived like Adam. In fact, it's precisely because Jesus saw through death's charade that he accepted death's embrace, that he cried out, "Not my will, but yours be done" (Luke 22:42 NIV). For when Christ looked at death, what he saw was us. What he saw was fallen, broken humanity. He didn't choose to unite with death; he chose to unite with us. For us, when the Word became flesh, God became accessible to death, even death on a cross. But, much to death's chagrin, the opposite is also true: death is now accessible to God.

RESTORING EDEN

From the cross (John's seventh sign), Jesus cries out, *"It is finished"* (John 19:30). What *is finished*? What is *complete*? The very next verse gives us a clue and a familiar invitation in John's Gospel—an invitation to count: "Now it was the day of Preparation, and the next day was to be a special Sabbath" (John 19:31 NIV). If "the next day" was the Sabbath, then Jesus's death on the cross occurs on the sixth day of the week—the same day humanity was created in Genesis 1. The sixth day of creation is followed by the seventh day, where God "rested from all the work he had done in creation" (Gen. 2:3b). He rested on day seven from all that he had *finished*— the same day Christ's body rested in the tomb from all that *he* had finished. A tomb, in John's Gospel, which happens to be located in a garden:

> At the place where Jesus was crucified, there was a
> garden, and in the garden, there was a new tomb
> (John 19:41).

John's Gospel starts "in the beginning," and here the Gospel approaches its end with an emphasis one can hardly miss:

(1) [where] "Jesus was crucified" = *union with death*
(2) "there was a garden" = *an image of Eden*
(2) [and] "in the garden" = *an image of Eden*
(1) "a new tomb" = *death repurposed for a new union*

119

Christ's death, like creation, ends in a garden, but *now* this garden contains a tomb. A "new" tomb. Not a tomb that returns its occupant to the dust like tombs of old, but a *new* tomb that returns humanity to life. Not a tomb that offers humanity union with death, but a *new* tomb that guides humanity to union with God. A *new* tomb that produces the fruit of a new life, the fruit of a resurrection; of Christ's resurrection, of our resurrection—humanity's return to a restored Eden, humanity's re-union with its Creator, humanity's redemption.

You see, God didn't choose the union with death; he chose union with humanity—humanity, since Genesis 3, "united" with death. This is why the only possible answer to Christ's query in the garden of Gethsemane—"My Father, if there is any other way, please take this cup of [death] away from me" (Matt. 26:39)[8]—is: "*No. You must die.*" Why? Because the good shepherd goes to where the lost sheep are.

And, for death, the results have been disastrous. On the tree between two trees, Jesus's final breath filled the container of death with the infiniteness of God, causing death to split wide open, spewing forth Christ as a firstborn from the gaping womb of death's tomb.[9] The incarnate Word's embrace of death pressed the finitude of death to its breaking point. As God in the flesh, Jesus pressed into death and, indeed, surpassed death's reach into hell itself (Ps. 139:8; 1 Pet. 3:19), only to reverse course through the grave, raised by the Spirit, in his glorious resurrection (Rom. 8:11) and, eventually, ascended into heaven to sit at God's right hand (Rom. 8:34), thereby writing a new ending to the one-flesh-with-death narrative, thereby completing humanity's creation left unfinished by Adam's fruit, thereby providing a path to union with God *through death.*

THE DEATH OF DEATH

Death could "unite" with humanity and increase in power, but it can't endure union with the incarnate God and stay the same. For in Christ, death has been transformed from a barrier segregating humanity *from* God into a gateway for humanity's union *with* God. As 1 Peter 3:18 celebrates, "For Christ also suffered once for sins, the righteous on behalf of the unrighteous, that he might *bring you to God.*" Jesus's sacrifice doesn't eliminate death; it doesn't overpower humanity's choice in Eden. Instead, Christ's cross *repurposes* death. So now, through the crucifixion of the Word-become-flesh, death can lead to life, death can lead to faithfulness, death can lead to union with God—*in Christ* (2 Cor. 5:21).

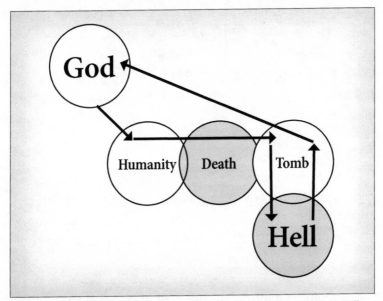

Christ's path of redemption: incarnation, "union with death," descent into hell, resurrection, ascension, and union with God

In Christ, humanity's narrative is liberated from un-creation, unfettered from the shackles of "union" with death, freeing us to follow Christ's path through death and beyond death to union with God—beyond the Fall to a "new tomb" through which we can "partake in the divine nature, having escaped the corruption in the world caused by sinful desires" (2 Pet. 1:4). *In Christ*, death now unites instead of separates, restores instead of divides, redeems instead of condemns. The cross of Christ inverts the narrative of Genesis 3 and undoes the tragedy of Genesis 4. The fruit of Adam's union with death at the forbidden tree was Cain's murder of Abel between two trees: Eve *loses* her son to death. The fruit of Christ's union with death at the tree between two trees produces the opposite—a mother *receives* a son through death:

> Jesus saw his mother [at the foot of the cross], and
> the beloved disciple standing nearby. He said to her,
> "Woman, behold your son," and, then, to the disciple, he
> said, "Behold your mother." And from that time on, the
> disciple took her into his own home. (John 19:26–27)[10]

In Christ, fear is no longer present, for death now leads to life instead of division. Death now leads to intimacy instead of isolation. Death now leads to union with God.

What *is finished*? Death's tyranny, death's futility, death's deception, death's un-creation. *In Christ*, self-preservation is no longer necessary. Violence is no longer useful. Hatred and unforgiveness are no longer sufficient, for love and mercy break forth in a new creation, peace and purity emerge from a "new tomb," the truth and the life are unearthed in the name of Jesus. The slain Lamb stands enthroned because the final breath of the incarnate Word repurposed death for union with God, transforming mutilation into restoration. The grotesque into the beautiful.

In Christ, and with Paul, all of creation can now sing:

> "Where, O death, is your victory?
> Where, O death, is your sting?" (1 Cor. 15:55 NIV)

LIFE IN THE EIGHTH DAY

Since Genesis 3, humanity has been caught in an endless cycle of seven days—day one ends as day two begins, day two leads into day three, and on and on until day seven ends, starting the cycle over with day one. An endless seven-day cycle imprisoned by the Fall; a seven-day cycle united to death, saturated in evil, spiraling in violence, decay, and despair. An endless Gethsemane where loneliness is a closer companion than community, where betrayal is more common than grace, where heaven seems to have abandoned earth. But after the Word-become-flesh cries out *"It is finished,"* the seven-day cycle is broken, and Christ ushers in a new day. A new dawn. A new creation. An eighth day, where the seven-day cycle no longer holds sway.

The morning of the resurrection, the garden "was still dark" (John 20:1), formless and void. Mary Magdalene saw the tomb but did not see that it was "new." She "stood outside the tomb crying" (John 20:11 NIV), unaware that she stood in an eighth day. Mary desperately sought her beloved, crying out like God in Eden, "Where are you? Where have they taken the body of my Lord?" Suddenly, she turned "and saw Jesus standing there," but still accustomed to darkness, "she didn't recognize it was him" (John 20:14). He was alive in the world, and "though the world was made through him" (John 1:10 NIV), Mary didn't recognize him. Instead, she mistook the Creator for a caretaker, "thinking he was just the gardener" (John 20:15). Thinking the seven-day cycle had reset to another day one. Yet in *this* garden, John offers an eighth sign that welcomes all of creation into an eighth day. A new garden, a new tomb, a new creation through Christ's resurrection.

Death as *we* know it no longer exists in Christ. No, death was not obliterated. Not forgotten. Not annihilated. But repurposed. Redeemed. In the eighth day, the Genesis narrative is inverted, dislodging the fruit of Adam and Eve. In the eighth day, death is life; death is resurrection; death is union with God—the "gardener" (John 20:15b). In the eighth day, death is defeated not because Christians now are able to bypass it, but because death now becomes the entry point to union *with* God instead of separation *from* God.

This life-in-the-eighth-day is what causes Paul to scream "By no means!" when answering the question "Shall we go on sinning so that grace may increase?" (Rom. 6:1–2 NIV). In Christ, the seven-day cycle of sin is no more; the grammar of death is no longer our native tongue. In Christ, an eighth day dawns, transforming death into a doorway to the divine so that humanity can become one with the God who became one with flesh. Union not through disobedience or sin like Adam, but through fidelity and purity like Christ—dying to the seven-day cycle so that we can live in an eighth day.

> For if we have become one with [Christ] in a death like his, we will certainly be united with him in a resurrection like his. For we know that our old self was crucified with him so that the body given to sin might perish, so that we no longer live as slaves to sin—because whoever has died has been set free from sin. (Rom. 6:5–7)

In Christ, death now leads to life. This is why Paul urges Christians "to present your bodies as a living sacrifice" (Rom. 12:1 ESV). This is why Paul boasts, "I have been crucified with Christ. I no longer live, but Christ lives in me" (Gal. 2:20). This is why Paul explains, "We always carry around in our body the death of Jesus, so that also the life of Jesus may be revealed in our body" (2 Cor. 4:10).

Life in the eighth day strips away death's deception, death's self-proclaimed sovereignty, opting instead for the new tomb found in Christ alone. In the eighth day, humanity responds to

Christ's call by taking up our cross, now knowing that "whoever wants to save their life [self-preservation] will lose it [like Adam], but whoever loses their life on account of me [self-denial] will find it [like Christ]" (Matt. 16:25). Knowing that through Christ, we can now receive the union we long for most: union *through death* with the God in whose image we were created.

Embracing Death to Find Life

Christ only embraced death because he saw us in it. And now we enter death because we see Christ, hanging on a tree between two trees. The *true* tree of life leading to a garden where death is subsumed into the wounds of the resurrected King. Wounds in his hands and his side that he invites us to inspect—"Put your finger here and look at my hands" (John 20:27a). Wounds that he invites us to enter—"Reach out your hand and put it into my side" (John 20:27b NIV). Why? So that we might "stop doubting and believe" (John 20:27c NIV). So that we might enter into an eighth day. So that we might become one with the Word who became one with us.

The resurrection teaches us that a new life in Christ doesn't merely erase the past, as if it no longer exists. It redeems the past, so that what did exist now exists in a completely different way. Yes, Jesus was resurrected into a new body, but it was *still* a body. Yes, Jesus's resurrected body was void of death, but it still preserved death's history in the holes of his hands and side. Similarly, the wounds of our past are not eradicated in Christ, but repurposed—experienced anew as scars, preserving the moment of our wounds in a visible celebration of our healing.

On occasion, I still think about Joe. The babysitter who gave me my wounds. But the thoughts occur less frequently than before and come with a much different tone. Sitting through hours of counseling, countless nights toiling, endless conversations talking and crying with friends and family, I've noticed a new fruit blossoming in the garden of my heart. As the healing rain gently falls from above, I've noticed my hatred seeping into the soil of my soul and mixing with a grain of wheat that fell into the earth and died (John 12:24). A blossom emerges, replacing my pain with hope. Replacing my anger with care. Replacing my hatred with love, joy, grace, and thankfulness. Thankful for a new life. Thankful for a resurrection, for an eighth day. Thankful for Joe.

Thankful for the wounds that have now become scars celebrating the healing power of Jesus. I find myself *not* wishing away any of the pain of the past, refusing the wine mixed with gall (Matt. 27:34), but instead, embracing death to find life. Entering the tomb to unite with Christ. And I pray the same for Joe.

I pray Joe finds redemption. I pray Joe finds life in Christ at the tree between two trees that leads to a plush new garden still containing a tomb. A *new* tomb offering a new self "renewed in full knowledge according to the image of its Creator" (Col. 3:10). I pray Joe finds healing from his wounds, so that one day, under the shade of the tree of life in the new Eden, sitting redeemed in Christ, we can come together in grace, celebrate the scars of our healing, and reminisce on days gone by when death used to divide. When death used to separate. When death used to be capitalized as "Death"—an insurmountable foe, a tyrannical leader, an impenetrable barrier that kept us from God and each other. That kept us from union and grace. That kept us from forgiveness and Christ.

Yet now, in this garden, for the boy and his babysitter, death is only a memory preserved in the scars of our healing—death transformed into a pathway to union with God. Through Christ. Because of Christ. *In Christ.*

I long for the day I can sit with Joe and say with Christ, "*It is finished.*"

This is atonement. This is salvation.

In Christ alone.

CHAPTER NINE

SEX
A Model of Divine Union

For God so loved the world . . .
—John 3:16

In the beginning, God created the cosmos, and called it good. In the Fall, humanity "united" with death, and moved east of Eden. But by God's grace, that's not the end of the story. Humanity's narrative doesn't progress from created-in-God's-image to united-with-Death-in-disobedience, ceasing to move forward, caught in Death's continuous seven-day cycle of un-creating tyranny. "For God so loved the world" (John 3:16), he became flesh, dwelled among them, and hung on a tree between two trees, honoring humanity's Edenic choice by becoming obedient to death. But death could not contain the infinite. Death could not retain a union birthed in obedience. Through Christ, death transformed. Death's womb burst forth with resurrection. Death was altered from a barrier that keeps humanity *from* God into the path of union *with* God.

"For God so loved the world . . . "

THE LOCATION OF LOVE

I'm not the first to ask the question, and I won't be the last to ask it today: Where is the location of love? Where is the clearest entry point to love? Where is the intersection of love and life—an intersection where I can stand and embrace this evasive union?

Like the mystic crossroads woven into the lyrics of blues lore, the intersection of love is mythic. The location of love elusive. Love seems to flit in and out of our lives on a cupid's wings, striking the unexpected and intoxicating the vulnerable—yet vanishes like a morning mist, refusing to reveal from whence it came and where it journeys next.

Between two trees, love's residence is unclear. Is it found in the songs of sirens? Is it found in the bravery of a knight charging the dragon to rescue the imprisoned princess? Is it found in the electricity of a first kiss or the intangibles of a last breath? Or is it found resting in clasped hands of faithful lovers? Does it hide in the sunset of the Rocky Mountains or in the wind caressing the Kansas meadows? Where is the location of love?

Even love's definition is difficult to uncover. For love is a mixture of possession and release; love longs to be held, but if it's held too tight, it deforms into something else. Love enjoys pursuit, yet is repulsed by suffocation. Love wants to be noticed, but wilts under too intent a gaze. Love plays that wretched game of hide-and-seek—content with either position in the game.

Love taunts only to increase desire. Love heals, transforming the wound into barely recognizable scars. Love can climax with sex, but refuses to be cheapened through infidelity or selfishness. Love rejects a price tag, but flutters to new heights in the presence of sacrifice. Love isn't measured by stock markets or monetary worth, but through measurements that defy calculation. That, in many ways, transcend our world completely.

Yet love is not completely out of reach.

The location of love is readily witnessed in the physical, in the flesh. A gentle touch in a moment of grief; a tender caress just before a passionate kiss. An arm around the shoulder eases pain; the footsteps of a parent dispel fear of the dark or anxiety of the unknown. Love invades our space, intersecting with what we can touch, hear, see. As John reminds, the cross itself offers us the physical presence of love:

> This is how we know what love is: Jesus Christ laid down his life for us. (1 John 3:16a NIV)

The cross elucidates and ignites the advances of love, which always contain a movement "toward." Limbs outstretched, bringing together what was separate—spanning the void with a movement *toward*. Not through a parasitic compulsion or necessity, as if the other completes what's lacking in us. Not to be captured—for possession is never the goal of love. But a movement *toward* with the intent of union. Not union through force, but through choice. In *choice*, the location of love emerges, offering transformation through union. *Willful* union.

THE DIVINE MYSTERY OF SEX

Why does Satan distort sex in every generation?

Why is it that six thousand years ago, sixty years ago, and sixty minutes ago are all saturated with satanic sexual perversion, pornography, and abuse? Sure, societies struggle with greed, violence, and lies, but sex usually holds a distinguished position of distortion—a unique target for Satan among many. But why?

In the United States, sex is currency used to buy and sell fidelity on the open market. Sex sells products, children, and love. Even when we know the love is a generic knockoff, we pay above full price. Even the homeless heroin addict knows that food and their next fix can be purchased with sex. Our culture is obsessed with sex.

But obsession with sex doesn't mean we understand it. Oftentimes obsession obscures the object (or subject) of our desire, exaggerating it to levels it can't sustain or diminishing it to extremes devoid of value. In our pursuit of "freedom," we've obliterated all boundaries that keep us from whatever versions of sex we can dream up, declaring war on fidelity and labeling monogamy as "unnatural." So sex becomes an instrument of self-expression and self-fulfillment, without even a passing nod at self-denial.

Sex before marriage is assumed; sex with multiple partners a given; abstinence or restraint of any kind is labeled outdated, impractical, and, once again, unnatural. From songs to screens to ads to headlines, sex saturates our society, inebriating our senses and divorcing us from any semblance of love, even peddling the lie that sex can "make love" with various shades of grey. The exaggeration of sex in our society directly results in the loss of true connection, true *union*, a true definition of *transformation*. For as sex increases in accessibility, our hope for "becoming someone different" diminishes in direct proportion.

Yet this is nothing new.

Ancient Greece decorated its public forums with disrobed deities, phallic utensils, and bosom décor. Rome housed temple prostitutes, orgy celebrations, and an emperor who married a castrated fourteen-year-old boy.[1] Sex is a persistent target for demonic distortions and deception, which should signal something to us about the significance of sex. For if Satan persistently twists a particular aspect of God's creation, it must contain a divine mystery that could lead to humanity's redemption and, still more, transformation.

Which raises the question: Why does Satan distort sex in every generation?

With equal vigor, though, God fights to keep sex pure. God spends a significant portion of Scripture commanding, exhorting, and vying for sexual purity. Sex is a favorite in biblical lists of prohibitions, from adultery to lust to homosexuality to bestiality to fornication to even just looking at a woman as a sexual object.[2] The purity of sex is paramount for God. Sexual infidelity is a chief metaphor for rebellion against God throughout the Old Testament: Psalm 50:16–18; Proverbs 7:1–27; Jeremiah 3:1–25; 9:1–2; 13:24–27; 23:9–14; Ezekiel 16:15–43; 23:1–49; and the entire book of Hosea. In Revelation, sexual immorality is three times coupled with "murder" in lists of repulsive acts by rebellious humanity (Rev. 9:21; 21:8; 22:15), accentuating God's earnestness. Time and again, God calls attention to sex, demanding pristine care and obedience.

At some point we need to ask, *Why?* Why does the Bible spend so much time discussing sex? Fighting for sexual purity? Rejecting sexual immorality?

Or the related question, "What are we losing in the church today by avoiding this topic of sex?" Sex plays an awkward role in our churches, usually shrouded in shame and sent to the parking lot to sit in the parked car in the sweltering heat. If we preach on sex, it's usually immersed in a negative tone or trivialized in a generic sermon from Song of Solomon. ("I mean, it's in the Bible," we lament. "I guess we have to preach from it sometimes.") In the church, sex is taboo. Something we don't discuss, and especially not a topic we want to read about in a book from a Christian publisher (sorry; not sorry). Yet if Satan spends so much time perverting sex and God spends so much energy trying to keep sex pure, what are we missing that the divine sees? What divine mystery embedded in sex are we overlooking?

Answer?

God and Satan target sex because they understand that sex is an essential tool for understanding the incarnation, for understanding transformation, for understanding divine union. Sex can illuminate humanity's problem ("union" with death) and Christ's redemption (union with God). In other words, as the climax of physical intimacy, sex is the clearest entry point to understanding the depths of union on any level, but especially with the divine. For sex is union. Sex is two becoming one flesh by willfully moving toward one another with the intent of union—with the purpose of the fullest extent of intimacy and vulnerability a physical body can conjure with its senses, and yet invokes that which moves beyond our senses. Even distortions of sex entice the onlooker, suggesting that perhaps love is located there. That perhaps something divine is present.

A Tale of Two Women

Let's approach the topic of "sex as union" through another question: Why does the destruction of the prostitute in Revelation 18 end with the wedding feast of the Lamb and his bride in Revelation 19? Why juxtapose these two women?

The image of the prostitute centers on sex as a "union" birthed through infidelity. No one questions the importance of sex to grasp the potency of the image, for even Revelation 17:2 and 18:3 make explicit what is already assumed, "The kings of the earth engaged in illicit sex (*porneia*) with her" (see also 18:9). The image of a prostitute invokes three key components further expounding the definition of "union" implicit in sex. First, prostitutes reduce sex to a currency where both parties come together (or "unite") in order to receive something from the other. The prostitute takes money; the visitor takes sex.

Second, this "union" is based on mutual selfishness. So long as sex (for the visitor) or money (for the prostitute) is secured, little concern is paid for the well-being of the other party. So, in Revelation 18:11, at the news of the prostitute's destruction, the merchants of the earth "wail and mourn over her," not because they love her or care for her, but "because no one buys their cargoes any longer" (Rev. 18:11). Selfishness is at the center of this sexual encounter, of this parasitic "union."

Third, the image of a prostitute connotes infidelity, or multiple sexual partners. This is found in the plural "kings" (Rev. 18:3) and in the occupational reality of a prostitute—more money is secured by servicing more clients than just one. With a prostitute, infidelity is assumed.

Thus, sex is central to the nuances of "union" with the prostitute in Revelation 18. The image doesn't just contain sex, but, indeed, depends on it, for sex with a prostitute is not just "union" but a particular type of "union." So why does the destruction of the prostitute in Revelation 18 end with the wedding feast of the Lamb and his bride in Revelation 19?

Given this juxtaposition with the prostitute, it's strange how our interpretations of Revelation 19 completely avoid factoring sex into the wedding imagery of the Lamb and his bride. To even suggest its presence is taboo and considered repulsive. But why center the conversation on sex with the prostitute in Revelation 18, yet completely uproot sex from the conversation in Revelation 19 when wedding imagery *is invoked*? For sex is as central to a wedding as it is to a brothel. Sex is the consummation of the wedding covenant—when the two "become one flesh" (Gen. 2:24).

We must remember, evil creates nothing. It can only distort what is already created by God and called "good." This goes for sex as well. Sex was not a result of Genesis 3. It existed in Eden before the Fall (Gen. 2:24). And it's no accident that when Adam and Eve became one flesh with death, they immediately covered up their nakedness in shame (Gen. 3:7). Why? Because union in any form, especially sex, had now been perverted by death's distortion. By death's deception. "Union" with death perverts sex into the self-serving act of the prostitute—a distortion absent in the wedding feast of the Lamb.

In Revelation 19, the bride (singular) has "made herself ready" adorned with "fine linen, bright and clean" (19:7–8 NIV), emphasizing her purity and, by extension, her fidelity. God intended this sexual purity to be brought to marriage by both parties, who then honor God by uniting in sex in order to *give* something to the other party: themselves—completely and without reservation. In contrast to the prostitute, this union is based on mutual self-denial, with the central concern for the other party's well-being in the act of union. Selflessness, then, is at the center of holy sexual union. A union rooted in mutual fidelity—pure virgins abstaining from union with other partners prior to this union and thereafter.

Thus, the marriage feast of the Lamb in Revelation 19 contrasts union with God and union with death (Rev. 18) *through* the imagery of sex. Union through fidelity is not the same as "union" through infidelity. "Union" for personal gain is not the same as union through self-denial. The prostitute and the bride provide a contrast that reveals the divine mystery of union that inevitably results in humanity's transformation—for better or worse.

PAGAN WORSHIP VS. DIVINE UNION
Now, the goal of this discussion isn't to be unnecessarily crass or to devolve the conversation into pagan practices envisioning sex with deities. It's about understanding the depths of union. It's about answering the question: Why does Satan go to such great lengths to distort sex and God go to such great lengths to preserve its purity? The answer is: Both of them understand the revelatory power of sex to communicate transformation as union with God.

Sex is creation's best effort to understand the depths of divine union—whether with God or with death. But our "union" with death prevents us from discussing this much further, because our distorted view of creation reduces the mystery of union into a pornographic physical act. Yet, we must remember, sex was something God created *before* the Fall; it's not a result *of* the Fall. The idea of two becoming "one flesh" (union) is in Genesis 2, not Genesis 3: "A man leaves his father and his mother and is *united* to his wife. They *become one flesh*" (Gen. 2:24). Sex was part of the creation that God called "good" (Gen. 2:23–25); it's only through death's distortion that shame and perversion deform this mysterious union.

Even after the Fall, though, sex is still the conduit through which life is created, because while death distorts sex, it hasn't destroyed its ability to connect us with life—for even in the midst of fallen creation, sex still births life. Sex still expresses love. And in the right context, sex can still be healing, a beautiful expression of reconciliation after a fight or a tender demonstration of fidelity and unity. And in the context of Christ, sex can become a powerful tool for teaching humanity about union with God, illuminating the incarnation and the Trinity itself.

In sex, "two become one" while still remaining *distinctly* two. Union without obliteration. This is exactly how the church has described Christ's incarnation throughout history: fully God and fully human interpenetrated in one person. A union that neither corrupts nor compromises the true divinity or the true humanity, yet unites them nonetheless. Similarly, comparable language is employed to describe the union of the Trinity: three persons, one being. Three distinct persons interpenetrated in eternal unity through selfless giving and receiving in one being.

The ability of sex to describe the incarnation, Trinitarian relation, and union with God provides, then, a necessary backdrop for God's zeal in protecting this sacred act. For when people engage in sex outside of marital fidelity, sex becomes a distorted amalgamation of multiple unions and divorces that move far beyond notches on a bedpost. Sex is union. Sex is an interweaving of not just the body but the soul. *This* is why divorce is so appalling to God—because it affirms infidelity, the breaking of a bond in which two had already become one. This is precisely the narrative of Genesis 3, where Adam and Eve ingested the fruit, spurned union with God, and instead interpenetrated with death itself. Infidelity. Divorce. Adultery. Union with someone other than God.

So, no, this discussion of sex is not crass, but a commitment to the belief that all of God's creation points to revelation of him. Even sex. And sex finds its pure pedagogy in the revelation of Jesus Christ—where relationships of a prostitute are supplanted by, replaced with, restored to relationships of bridal beauty and fidelity in the wedding feast of the Lamb.

TRANSFORMATION AS UNION WITH GOD

When sex is redeemed in Christ, wrested from the clutches of prostitution with death, *transformation* is unveiled as *union with God*. Union in which two become one without the loss of the two. For the joining of two persons doesn't obliterate the individuality of either, but births a union surpassing what the violence of death can attain or imagine.

When we truly understand the mystery of "two becoming one flesh," we begin to conceive of divine depths of *transformation* far beyond anything physical: For what is the Lord's Supper through the lens of union—from the view of two becoming one flesh? What does it mean to be the "body of Christ" from the vantage point of two becoming one flesh? What does it mean for a human author to write Scripture inspired by the Holy Spirit from the perspective of two becoming one flesh? Or how do we understand the new heaven and the new earth in Revelation 21 through this mystery of divine union: two becoming one flesh? Or what about Christ giving the Spirit to his disciples by "breathing" on them (John 20:22), like God at creation breathing into the nostrils of man "the breath of life" (Gen. 2:7)? Or what does two becoming one flesh teach us about the indwelling of the Holy Spirit in all Christians (James 4:5)? Or about the promise for Christians to "partake in the divine nature" (2 Pet. 1:4)?

What does sex teach us about transformation?

Transformation is union with God. Becoming "one flesh" with God. As Christ condescended from heaven to earth, uniting his divinity with our humanity, incarnating the invisible God, so too is our transformation an ascension from earth to heaven, uniting our humanity with his divinity.

Before Protestants start screaming "Heresy!" in a chant that drowns out the "Amens!" of the Eastern Orthodox, listen to Paul describe this mystery in Ephesians 5:28–32:

> Husbands ought to love their wives as their own bodies. (NIV)

Why? Because husbands and wives are *one flesh.*

> The one who loves his wife loves himself. For no one ever hated their own body, but he nourishes it and cherishes it, just as also Christ does the church. For we are members of his body.

Then Paul, seemingly at random, quotes Genesis 2:24 from the creation account:

> For this reason a man leaves his father and his mother and is *united* to his wife, and *the two become one flesh.*

So far so good. No controversy on the horizon. Husbands and wives united together in sex, where two become one flesh. But in the very next sentence, Paul reveals his true reason for quoting Genesis 2:24—union with God:

137

This is a profound mystery, for I am talking about Christ and the church.

Let's follow this astounding progression: (1) Husbands, treat your wife as your own body. Why? (2) Because in marriage, two become one flesh. Not merely a contractual agreement. Not merely a legal document. But two becoming one flesh. Why does this matter? (3) Because, Paul says, the same is true for Christ and the church. Through Christ, we become "one flesh" with the divine.

BEYOND THE DISTORTION

It's impossible to understand transformation with the current state of sex in our society. Transformation is cheap, prostituted in self-help books, participation trophies, and Hollywood-ized by tummy tucks and breast enhancements aimed at increasing sex appeal. Our view of sex damns our definition of transformation before we even start.

In today's society, we normalize promiscuity, but love expects fidelity. Love assumes self-denial. Love supposes mutual acceptance, mutual embrace, mutual trust, mutual sacrifice. All woefully rare in today's world.

Sex without *mutual, willful* union doesn't beget love, only treachery—a parasitic union comparable to death. We must move sex beyond this distortion, this deception of death, and reclaim its place in Genesis 1–2, where male and female were created in God's image, interpenetrated by the eternal Trinity, "predestined to be conformed to the image of God's Son" (Rom. 8:29).

But ultimately, this isn't about sex at all. It's about union. Death. Incarnation. Redemption. Resurrection. Re-union with God in Eden.

It's about the beginning of transformation.

SECTION FOUR

THE LIGHT OF THE TREE OF LIFE

CHAPTER TEN

Opening the Womb to Truth
Union through *Kenosis*

I wake up each morning to a mirror. And I'm not sure I like it.

Even though sleep is a refreshing tool (at least most nights), my reflection in the mirror tells a different tale—puffy eyes, disheveled hair, and new zits so large they're demanding adoption papers. Even after I brush my teeth and my hair and put on fresh clothes, I look into the mirror only to find resilient disappointment staring back. Imperfections taunt me through disobedient hair cowlicks and new shades of gray in my beard and in my mane.

Yep, waking up to a mirror is a drab affair, but reflections don't end as I emerge from the bathroom—they increase in regularity and surprise. I warm up my breakfast and catch a glimpse of my reflection in the microwave doubling as a mirror. I pick up my phone and find my reflection there. I glance up at the blank TV and find my reflection even there. As I leave the house, reflections follow. I get into my car and, like a responsible driver, I check all of my *mirrors*: rear, sides, pull-down, child spy—all different shapes, sizes, and successes.

Reflections unending.

Relationships are like mirrors, which is probably why many long for them and yet are equally repulsed by the thought. Whether

141

we're talking about friends, mentors, or the almighty marriage, all relationships are mirrors offering opportunities for transformation. I tell my college students frequently, "Marriage is not a *corrective* for your flaws. Marriage is a big mirror that *exposes* your flaws." For when you're married, you realize just how selfish you truly are, just how impatient you truly are, just how set in your ways you actually are. How incapable you are of loving unconditionally and forgiving freely. How insensitive you are to another's pain, yet incredibly sensitive to a misplaced word or a misconstrued glance. And when you have kids? The mirror just gets bigger, and you realize you're actually worse off than you thought.

I suspect this is why divorce rates seem to outpace marriage covenants, especially after the arrival of a child. Eventually, people simply get tired of looking into the mirror, and instead of doing the hard work of transformation, they decide to trade in the old mirror for a newer model. Blaming the mirror for the poor reflection.

Indeed, reflections abound.

In the house, outside the house, driving, texting, with friends, with kids, in marriage, and even in Scripture itself—reflective surfaces are everywhere. The problem isn't finding one; the problem is sometimes mirrors reveal more than we care to see.

Interpretation as "I Don't Know"

Scripture doesn't always play by our list of interpretative rules. Thank God. We overconfidently flaunt our list of exegetical principles and cry, "Just follow my lead, and *I* will lead you to the author's truly and only intended meaning." That's bold, and borderline ridiculous. It trivializes the complexities of not just the depths of writing and communication but even the depths of God. I mean, how is it that a set of literary tools can exhaust the expanse of the eternal Word of God? As if our interpretative principles transform into some sort of infallible guide to mine the physical and spiritual aspects of a text as unfathomable as the leagues of the ocean—offering caves for spelunkers, treasures for conspiracy theorists, and brave new worlds for those patient enough and adventurous enough to dive deeper than the tanks of air can promise safe return. How is it that we are able to tame such a Leviathan? How is it that we are able to commandeer such a marvelous fortune of divine mystery?

Scholars are more likely to say "I love you" to one another than "I don't know." Both phrases are three words; both begin with a single letter; both have three syllables. Yet the latter is infinitely more rare in academia. Conspicuously so.

"I don't know" is synonymous with embarrassment in academic circles. We are researchers, professional thinkers who pride ourselves on bookworm features and knowing quite a lot about a lot. Thus to admit ignorance is an occupational hazard to be avoided like a leather suit at a water park. Many academics receive the words "I don't know" as a white flag of surrender—as if the onslaught of a fellow soldier's inquiry was simply too much to bear. In the academy, "I don't know" is spoken with a shiver in the voice and a quiver in the spine. With a pocket full of posies, scholars write papers, bloat footnotes, and scour monographs to mercilessly fend off the plague of "I don't know." For to utter these words is to admit a failure of calling—or so the story goes.

Some may find this narrative appalling, accusing scholars of arrogance or worse. Yet I've found that "I don't know" is equally rare outside of academia. Politicians dodge it like a donkey avoids an elephant; Facebook rants mock it as threads unravel with rubbish and no substance. Preachers can't admit it, engineers won't approach it, and social activists won't concede it. Science and the modern world tirelessly toil to eradicate these three words from our collective vocabulary. Through reason (empirical or rational), the scientific method, and federal grants, every "I don't know" is targeted with ruthless exaction. As knowledge increases, so does our arrogance, pretending that I-don't-know's tenuous existence is marching ever closer to its end.

When I look in the mirror, though, I find I'm no different. I confidently stride into the future aiming to conquer "I don't know," envisioning this quest as the majestic fruit of innovation, exploration, and creativity. I stubbornly shun "I don't know," opting instead for the deception of absolute knowledge. This assault, though, is nothing new. It's actually quite ancient. For Adam and Eve, reaching for the fruit from the tree of the knowledge of good and evil, were the first to compose the chords of disdain for "I don't know," a song humanity's been singing ever since.

It's just surprising to hear the tune still sung by so many of us Christians. We fill our sanctuaries and sermons with phrases that taunt "I don't know." We pronounce the eulogy of these three words through Communion meditations and special music. But we unwittingly assail the very thing we desire.

If we lose the ability to say "I don't know," we lose the ability to perceive mystery. A tragedy quite perilous to any society or individual, for to lose mystery is to forfeit the ability to see ourselves clearly. A rabbi was once asked, "Teacher, why do you keep the dietary laws?" Without pause, he responded, "Because *I don't know* what they mean."

"How foolish!" we mock.

"How deceived!" we accuse.

"Crucify blind faith!" we chant.

But "I don't know" isn't tantamount to ignorance or unintelligence. It's an admission of the existence of something beyond our self. An acknowledgment of the limitations of our knowledge, our ability to perceive, our capacity to understand. "I don't know" is a commitment to pursuit, an awareness that anything of true value is infused with elements of divine mystery—infused not just for a time, but ever and always. "I don't know" is to approach the Scriptures gratefully, humbly, knowing who we are, knowing who God is, and embracing the grace that makes such an interaction possible.

"I don't know" cleanses us of ourselves, positioning us to receive more of the One we simply don't know. The One that cannot be known, yet *is* known. Known only through his desire to be known. Known only through his movement toward us, through his revelation, both in creation and in Scripture. The infinite, incorruptible God shrouded in mystery, yet unveiled in the "I don't know." But unveiled only to the extent that the I AM *entrusts* and that humanity is able to *receive*. To receive, that is, through transformation into the image of the I AM.

The Mold of Mary

To receive the Word of God, whether in interpretation or transformation, we need to become more like Mary: the Mother of God. For many Protestants, anti-Catholic biases go hand in hand with anti-Mary sentiments, both of which, as a Protestant, I deeply lament. Sure, I know the stories of the indulgences and the alleged bravery to wrest the gospel from the grip of the papacy largely attributed to Ninety-Five Theses and the declaration "Here I stand, I can do no other, so help me God." But that was five hundred years ago. The Hatfields and the McCoys have ended feuds quicker. Not to mention, we Protestants conveniently overlook the point that the entire movement was called a "Re-formation." Not a "segregation." But, alas, the unity movement running in my blood carries me away yet again.

Back to the issue at hand: Mary.

Sure, I'm uncomfortable with the level of exaltation Mary has received by the Catholic church, but I'm equally uncomfortable with Protestants treating her just like any other woman. Usually just ignoring her altogether. I can't even remember the last time I heard Mary's name mentioned in a Protestant church service outside of another rendition of Mark Lowry's *Mary, Did You Know?* Which is alarming. The song, yes, but I mean the absence of Mary in the Protestant church. This is the woman who carried the Word of God in her womb. This is the woman who gave birth to the Creator of the universe. Who breast-fed Immanuel. The woman whose fingers Jesus clutched as a child eager to walk. The woman who sat the Wisdom of God on her lap when he scraped his knee, wiping tears from his eyes and holding him close with the tenderness only a mother can offer. This is the woman who nurtured the Light of the world into manhood and sat at the foot of the cross. This is Mary: the Mother of God.

As a Protestant, I refuse to ignore her any longer. For without the presence of Mary in our theology, how can we even approach the Word of God, more or less house it in our interpretative womb? I mean, how many of us, *like Mary*, can claim a holiness sufficient to host the Word of God *in us*, and as a teenager, no less? My teenage years were anything but hospitable to the holiness of God. My teenage years were more akin to traversing a minefield hoping to minimize the damage and not leave maimed or worse. And working with college students as an occupation, I'm reminded consistently that I'm not alone.

I was selfish as a teenager. Angry as a teenager. Arrogant, isolated, impatient, and self-seeking. Yet, as a teenager, Mary was filled with grace and humility. Possessing a pious resilience unto herself so fierce that all of creation could be blessed through her womb—through her Son. When we peer into the face of the unassuming heroine, we see the radiant image of God. Majestic even. We see the divine strategy of union *through* emptying.

Union through *Kenosis*

It's easy to blame the mirror for the poor reflection. On our path through Gethsemane, carrying our cross on the road to transformation, it's easy to accuse the reflective surface of distortion when in reality we're the problem. At times, contained in a convicting passage of Scripture or the gentle rebuke from the Holy Spirit, we see our reflection in the mirror clearly: strengths, weaknesses, gifts, pitfalls, talents, temptations, sins, successes, flaws, failures. Everything. Two options, then, lie within our reach: transformation of us (the image in the mirror) or distortion of him (the image of God). And typically, we trend toward the latter.

When confronted with transformation, we often change the Word, the image of God, to match our reflection. Instead of a crucified peasant carpenter, he becomes a white, middle-class Republican ready to launch a war on his enemies either in retaliation or as a preemptive strike, all in the name of protecting his interests at home or abroad in Jerusalem, Judea and Samaria, or the ends of the earth. The image in the mirror, though, stares back as if it has a will of its own, counter to ours, challenging ours, inviting us to transform into the image of God reflected in the sacred text. Inviting us to deny ourselves, take up our cross, and follow the Word.

In order to receive the Word of God, we must be willing to empty ourselves of ourselves, just as Christ did. Just as Mary did. As discussed above,[1] Philippians 2:6–7 narrates the incarnation, describes Christ emptying himself to unite with flesh:

> Christ Jesus: Who, being in the form of God, did not regard equality with God something to be grasped; but he *emptied* (*kenosis*) himself, taking the form of a slave, being made in human likeness.

147

The Greek word *kenosis*, translated "emptied," invokes the simple principle of "How can I carry *those* groceries unless I put down *these* groceries filling my hands?" *Kenosis* is a carving out of space to create a greater capacity to receive. A greater capacity for union.

In order to become one flesh with God, we must become less, so that he can become more (John 3:30). Like Mary, we must commit to a posture of receptivity, allowing the Trinity to fill us with the Word, regardless of the end. For as the Spirit approached this teenage girl, there was a cavernous capacity to receive the totality of God in her womb. A divine humility to allow God to create once more, as he did "in the beginning," something out of nothing. A divine opportunity for the Wisdom of God to enter the world through unexpected and unassuming means: Christ born of a virgin.

Mary is a collision of activity and passivity, of work and grace. Mary enacts God's emptying (activity; work), which results in a union with God embodied in her womb (passivity; grace). Mary's emptying of herself to receive the Word of God is the essential point of intersection between her and Christ, and indeed, between us and the Word become flesh.

The mystics, ancient and modern, speak of the same emptying process in contemplative prayer. Not becoming nothing or a sort of ceasing to exist, like Zen, but emptying in order to receive— surrender of self to God himself to receive the Word itself. This is the complete opposite of seizing, possessing, grasping—the complete opposite of the Greek word *harpagmos* translated in Philippians 2:6 as "something to be grasped" or "something to be forcibly seized for selfish gain." "Emptying" (or *kenosis*) is the complete opposite of Adam and Eve in Genesis 3, *seizing* the fruit to grasp equality with God. *Kenosis* purges forcefulness, refuses ourselves, our advantages, our profits, and instead resiliently chooses to receive whatever God may give—something along the lines of "not my will, but yours be done" (Luke 22:42 NIV).

In fact, mystics like John of Patmos, John of the Cross, or Adrienne von Speyr speak of their visions in Marian terms—a reception of the divine Word through emptying of themselves. Mary-like *kenosis*: an essential entry point to receiving God's revelation, to receiving Christ's transformation. Why? Because we cannot receive God if we insist on rejecting God through choosing ourselves. We must, like Christ, deny ourselves, creating a greater capacity to receive union, so that, like Mary, our womb can be filled with the Word of God to birth God's message of grace. Or, in other words, we must deny the image of death and reclaim the image of God, within which we were created "in the beginning."

THROUGH THE EYES OF GOD

Out of all the mirrors and reflective surfaces that invade my life, I appreciate passenger-side mirrors the most. Why? Because they have the courage to confess what all other mirrors try to suppress: "objects in mirror are closer than they appear"—a roundabout way of admitting that mirrors distort reality. Sure, mirrors reflect reality, but not without alteration, inversion, or distortion. Even in a basic mirror, everything is inverted. What's *left* in my world is *right* for the image staring back at me, and vice versa. Mirrors can distort, mirrors can ensnare, and at times, mirrors can disorient.

For centuries, mirrors have tormented societies with superstition and vanity. In ancient civilizations, mirrors were, on occasion, banished because of accusations of divination. Mirrors haunt, distort, entice, disorient. Even for me, I must admit, a tinge of fear arises as I look in a mirror, hoping against hope that when I move, my reflection actually moves with me (further evidence of my neurosis, I'm sure).

Typically, though, mirrors terrorize us through subtle nudges toward vanity. Many are obsessed with what they see in a mirror and desire to see it again and again. We walk down city streets appearing to look in shop windows, but in reality, trying to catch another glimpse of our image. If someone catches our vain "window shopping," we pretend something's stuck between our teeth. Sure, for those cosmetic moments, mirrors can be a helpmate, but by and large, mirrors distort reality, ensnare us in narcissism or its equally powerful opposite, shame. Blinding us to the true image of ourselves: the Word of God.

I have a hard time accepting the Lord's acceptance of me. Not every moment of every day, or even every day. But on average, I'm more repulsed by the blackness of my heart than encouraged. More frustrated with my foolish choices than proud. Which is something I'm not proud to admit and not excited to write about for more than just me to see.

Several months ago, I was praying to the Lord and these very thoughts saturated the groans of my heart. Closing my eyes only caused the grief to increase, because unlike the mirrors in our homes, the mirrors of our souls enlarge when our eyes are shut. In shame, I cried out to the Lord, hoping the disgust I felt would be received as some sort of perverse offering. Suddenly, the Spirit carried me into God's throne room with Jesus standing to my left with a relaxed smile. I looked up toward the One seated on the imposing throne. Brilliant with light, his glory simply caused me to tremble. In shame, I lowered my head and saw that I was naked. No clothes to hide me, no fabric to conceal me, no fig leaves to obstruct. I was naked before the Lord and overwhelmed with disgust at the sight of *me*.

Suddenly, the perspective of the vision shifted from my eyes to the view from the One seated on the throne. As he gazed in my direction, from his perspective, I wasn't shamefully naked but glowing with the same brilliant light as him—swallowed in his radiant glory. The image shifted, once again, back to my perspective, but when I looked down, all I saw was repulsive nakedness. Once more, the vision moved to God's perspective, and I, once again, was shining like pure metal, radiant with his light. As the Spirit moved behind and through me, I received a sentence from the Lord much like receiving a wrapped present at Christmas (the entire object received all at once, yet more contained therein): "This is how I view you," he said. "To me, this is who you are."

THE EMPTY TOMB

The path of transformation reflects the positives and negatives of a mirror. Transformation is peering deeply into the mirror of our souls, struggling to look long enough for needed adjustments, yet aware of the dangers of distortion. At times, like an anorexic, we look into the mirror of our souls and all we see is bloated regret staring back. Sin done to us or by us. Shame mocking the perversion of God's image in us. Our past distorting our present. At other times, we're plagued with the inverse: We look at our souls and all we see is our accomplishments, puffing us up, making us appear holier than we truly are. Both extremes distort the image, obscure Christ in us, hide God's brilliant light behind our shameful nakedness.

I'm coming to realize that union with the Lord necessitates emptying myself of myself because I don't see myself clearly. My self-lashing, my proud boasting, my shame, my arrogance all fill me with *me*, leaving little room to receive another, more or less the infinite Creator. Like Christ, like Mary, to become one flesh with God, to unite with the divine, to transform into the image of the Word of God, I must embrace *kenosis*. I must commit to becoming less, so he can become more. I must surrender to the Spirit's power to empty me as it emptied the tomb.

CHAPTER ELEVEN

PERMISSION
The Path to Transformation

*I stand at the door and knock. If anyone hears
my voice and opens the door, I will come in and
eat with that person, and they with me.*

—Revelation 3:20

This text bothers me. Annoys me. I don't know, maybe I'm being too sensitive. But the text strikes me as slightly disingenuous. I mean, why would a sovereign God ever need to knock? Why would he ever need wait at any door before entering? Why not just use the "almighty" in his name and *enter*? Not waiting for someone to open it or invite him in, but just *enter* because he wants to? Why should *he*, the Creator of heaven and earth, wait for *us* to rise from our chairs, unlock the bolted door, and grant him entrance? Why should *he*, the Alpha and Omega, the Beginning and the End, the Great I AM delay moving into whatever location *he* desires whenever *he* desires? Why does Jesus need to knock at all?

My angst betrays my ignorance. Something I've grown accustomed to.

A friend of mine used to be a gangbanger in inner-city Indianapolis. His older brothers showed him the path of violence

153

and gang life, and, for a time, he was in prison for bashing the head of a rival gang member on a curb during a particularly tense moment. Story after story of his life before Christ provided more and more contrast to the man I saw standing before me—a clean-cut, articulate, loving husband and father of two wonderful children.

At one point, I shook my head and said, "I can't *believe* that's your story. I mean, I look at you and . . . it's just hard for me to believe that was you."

Without hesitation and so much as a smirk, he fired back, "Don't you believe in the resurrection?"

Puzzled, I nodded. "Well, yeah, but . . ."

"Then why's it so hard to believe in transformation?"

Why, indeed.

THE PUZZLE OF PERMISSION

"I stand at the door and knock."

According to texts like Revelation 3:20, transformation is immersed in a divine mystery of partnership. Of permission. Apparently there's something formative in our invitation, something revolutionary in our choice, something powerful in our permission that opens new avenues of interaction with the sovereign Lord. A power easy to overlook. A power easy to take for granted. A power not typically handled with much care.

Permission: a mystery as vast as the incarnation.

Not that we engage it as such. Not that we approach permission with the same reverence, recognizing the power it possesses. Oftentimes, we view permission as a mere formality; something to be sought, for sure, but not something containing much significance. Permission is something that if you have it, fine, but if not, there's always a way around it. In fact, our aversion to, or at least uneasiness with, permission reveals an awful lot about our relationship with force—for we simply don't think permission is always necessary.

"No trespassing" signs are seen as suggestions in the heat of the moment, especially if attached to a dare. "Go ahead," your idiot friend provokes. "I dare you to run up to the house and turn the doorknob." Desire and a dare easily move us beyond the search for permission and into the realm of force. This assumption, this impulse is why public service announcements have recently taken great pains to articulate that when a woman says no, the answer is no, even if, as despicable perpetrators protest, "She seemed to enjoy it."

Permission is sacred. Even if we treat it profanely. Even if we overlook the power it possesses. The mystery it contains. The divinity it emanates. To give permission to another is a moment charged with intimacy, a gesture suffused with intensity. For permission is an invitation to closeness. Permission reroutes the boundaries of our world to include another, to welcome another, to incorporate another into what is by design our own.

Permission is the climax of the preceding "choice." We are confronted with choices every single day—what clothes to wear, what toothpaste to buy, what plate to eat from, what product to put in our hair, what flavor to put in our coffee, what route to take to work, what speed we go to get there, what parking space to fill, what expression to use to greet a passerby, or whether to just ignore them altogether. We choose when we go to bed, when we wake up, what show we watch, what book we read, what store we shop at, what food we buy, what credit card we use, how much money we spend, and on and on it goes: our choices grant permission. Every day, we negotiate permission, using our divine gift of choice to, well—choose.

Yet somehow we forget the potency of permission that accompanies each and every choice we make. An omission that obscures not just texts like Revelation 3:20, but also distorts our view of how transformation works altogether.

A MOMENT VS. A MOVEMENT

Transformation isn't a moment; it's a movement.

You can't point back to an instance, to a single event, to a moment in time and say, "There! That's the moment of my transformation!" No. Transformation is more like a river than a cup of water. More like a forest than a lone tree. Sure, each movement is a series of moments, but no single moment contains the entire movement, just like no single frame contains the entire motion picture. The film is the movement of the moments, strung together with an intelligence guiding its end. And transformation is no different.

Each class of each semester, I spend about a week or so going through the syllabus. Not because I think students don't know how to read. I trust that by the time they get to college they have at least a serviceable capacity for literacy. But because, from the very beginning, I want to set a tone of clarity, expectations of high quality, and a context of trust—offering help with questions, prayers for struggles, and negotiations over frivolous assignments. I offer rationale for my "no screens in the classroom" policy, why I more than bristle at plagiarism, and other morsels of wisdom that don't always find their way into lectures.

Usually during this time I will, at some point, make this declarative statement (commonly with a flare of dramatic gravitas): Every choice you make, you become someone different. Every single choice you make, you become someone else. Whether or not to come to class is a choice that transforms you into someone. Whether or not to procrastinate on an assignment is a choice that transforms you into someone. Whether or not you choose to cheat on a paper or on a memory verse, you choose to become someone.

No, this isn't an exaggeration or some elaborate professorial ruse to guilt my students into compliance. This declaration is rooted in a firm belief that transformation isn't a moment, it's a movement. For, by God's design, we are always in a constant state of transformation, and that's something we don't get to choose. But what we do get to choose is who we become.

THE REFLECTION OF MY HEART

For years I've been fascinated by Hitler. Now, stay with me. I didn't say "admired," for, like anyone with any semblance of a conscience, I find Hitler's actions and legacy repulsive. Incomprehensible. An evil so perverse that his name is rightly placed alongside the despicable antagonists of history like Nero, Vlad II, Stalin, and others.

Yet Hitler fascinates me because he has emerged in our modern world as the archetypal symbol of evil—an embodiment of Satan himself. My intrigue, then, was guided by this line of inquiry: What creates someone this insufferable? This evil? What happened in this man's life that produced this unspeakable result? What event produced a life forever associated with evil?

So I picked up the biographical work by Ian Kershaw called *Hitler*, a 1,030-page tome, and began my search.[1] About halfway through the book, my wife asked me: "So, what have you learned so far? Anything interesting?"

I thought for a moment and said, "Yeah, two things. First, Hitler had daddy issues."

He was really close to his mom, but his relationship with his father was strained and characterized by intense conflict. Hitler simply never lived up to the dreams and demands of his father. After his mom died in 1907, Hitler, at the age of twenty, lived on the streets, homeless. In World War I, with nothing to lose, Hitler joined the army and found the family and acceptance he never had at home in his fellow soldiers. After World War I and Germany's defeat, the nation was left in rubble, once again leaving Hitler without a "father." Instead of street wandering, he turned to hatred, blaming, and the restoration of Germany—the resurrection of his "family." Hitler had daddy issues.

I stopped, looking down at the book and committing to silence, when my wife interjected: "Wait, you said *two* things. What's the other one?"

"Well," I hesitated. "Ummm . . . the second thing is tough . . . to say out loud. It actually kinda bothers me."

"Oh, come on," she laughed, questioning my high-maintenance drama. "Just tell me."

"All right—well . . . the more I read about Hitler . . . the more I see myself in him."

I was as shocked as the look on her face. I mean, I thought I would study him, find the source of his repulsive evil, and understand not just how to avoid it but how great the contrast is between him and me. But the more I read, the more I thought, "I get it."

Pain causes us to flail and lash out, to compromise who we are or who we want to be in exchange for another. And, deep down in the shadows of my heart, I kept thinking that if I was in his situation, I could see the darkness of my soul guiding me to respond in the same way. Which is overwhelming. Frightening. Embarrassing.

This realization scared me no end. I mean this guy is *pure* evil. This guy mercilessly killed six million Jews, not including the countless other people murdered in multiple wars both at home and abroad. This guy is the embodiment of Satan—a person appearing alongside Judas on people's top ten list of candidates for hell. Yet, here I am, studying his life and seeing a mirror into my own, coming to the startling conclusion: I'm not as different as I thought—or as I hoped.

Every decision we make, we become someone else. Every choice we embrace, we choose who we become. Nothing is wasted.

Nothing discarded. Every choice, every word, every accusation, every apology, every single decision we make, we become someone different.

A Dance with the Divine

So, who are you becoming?

This isn't a question consigned to the moment of conversion, as if transformation were a moment instead of a movement. It's a question asked and answered every instant of every day by Christian and non-Christian alike, whether we acknowledge it or know it. We are in a constant state of becoming, a neverending dance with transformation where, by God's design, *we lead*. We even get to choose our partner at the ball filled with many suitors, including Christ. Thus, sin is more frightening than just "Will I get into heaven or not?"; sin is a movement of transformation. A deliberate invitation to link arms with death to dance the night away.

Being in ministry for over fifteen years, I've seen my fair share of ministers fall into marital unfaithfulness. With an intern, with a secretary, with another minister on staff, with a volunteer in their ministry, with a fragile heart they were counseling—all of which come from real-life examples at the forefront of my mind right now. Minister after minister, they compromise their calling and unite with death through infidelity. But I stress to my students: The adultery *didn't begin* when the minister locked eyes with the secretary for the first time. It began fifteen years earlier when they decided to cheat on a test, when they chose to lie on a book report. It began fifteen years earlier when they embraced lies and deceit a choice at a time. And gradually, they became someone different. They became someone capable of shattering a marriage and ruining a ministry; they became another casualty of adultery.

From the perspective of permission, sin matures, taking on a new dimension and a greater seriousness, extending far beyond just whether or not I'm guilty of some indiscretion. No, sin becomes a conscious choice to grant death permission to enter your space and dine with you. Sin becomes a conscious choice to transform into an image other than God's. Sin, therefore, separates you from God, but not in location or space. Sin separates you from God on the level of being, on the level of essence, on the level of identity—for sin grants *permission* to unite you with death. Sin transforms you into something less than the image of God that produces fruit far different from the tree of life.

Until we embrace this definition of sin, we will continue to misdiagnose the problem and overlook the danger of our dance with death. So, for example, I sometimes get asked, "Is it a sin to watch an R-rated movie?" As a recovering legalist, I understand where this question comes from. This question is birthed from a view of God that depicts him as an overzealous director of heaven's HOA (Home Owner's Association), always looking for a loophole to keep people out of the pearly gates to ensure the property value increases with each new resident. In other words, behind the question "Is it a sin to watch an R-rated movie?" is a deeper concern about the identity of God: "Will he damn me for watching an R-rated movie? Will he keep me out of heaven for watching this film? Will God send me to hell because of this movie to prevent me from muddying the streams of living water with my communicable disease?"

But that's *not* who God is. That's *not* the God revealed throughout Scripture. Jesus, the "image of the invisible God" (Col. 1:15 NIV), didn't come looking for unique ways to keep people *away* from God but opened up scandalous avenues laden with immeasurable grace to draw *all* people into God's embrace (John 3:16). To woo all of creation into the transformative dance with the Trinity.

So, no. Watching an R-rated movie will not damn you.

But if sin is a movement of transformation (or better still: de-formation), then the question needs to shift. It's not "If I watch R-rated movies, will I be damned?" but "If I watch R-rated movies, who will I become?" Will you become more like Christ or less? This changes the question from conversion to discipleship, from the starting line to the race, from entrance into a location (heaven) to transformation into a person (Christ).

From a moment to a movement.

Transformation is inevitable, impossible to prevent. But the result is governed by *our* choices. With *our* permission. Therefore, we need not ask "Am I changing?" but instead "Who am I becoming?"

DINING WITH THE DIVINE

In Revelation 3:20, Jesus intentionally connects *permission* with another sacred act: eating.

> If anyone hears my voice and opens the door, I will
> come in and *eat with that person*, and they with me.

We eat so much we fail to see the divine revelation therein. Meals, like permission, are transformative. What you eat transforms you into someone different. Or, as some say it, "You are what you eat." Why? Because eating is granting permission, a choice of transformation. With every bite, whether healthy or not, you are choosing to unite yourself with something and, therefore, become someone different. Eating is sacred because it enacts the divine mystery of union—both in *what* you eat and *who* you eat with.

This reminds me of the lunch hour at middle school cafeterias—a nauseating mixture of plastic-like food and minefields of identity and insecurity. Whether you walk into the lunchroom with a sack lunch in hand or you exit the lunch line with a tray in tow, the cafeteria is terrifying for middle-schoolers who, by their body's uncomfortable reminder, are in a crucial time of transformation. Peering over the bustling tables, the awkward preteen intuitively knows that *who* they sit with, they become. If you sit with the "cool kids" and aren't humiliated to the point of retreat, then you become a part of them; you are one of them. Your identity changes. But if you sit down with the outcasts (or even more awkwardly, the outcasts come and sit down by you), then you become one of *them*. Regardless of who you *were*, now your identity is "outcast."

Identity and transformation are infused at mealtimes, transforming it into a daily reminder of the divine dance of transformation. A constant reminder of permission.

On the night of his betrayal, Jesus sat down with his disciples at a meal. A meal now present at the heart of Christian identity; a supper at the center of Christian worship. For that meal wasn't just for the disciples, at *that* time, for *that* moment. No, each Sunday, Jesus chooses anew to sit and eat with us. To come into our sanctuary, sit down at our table, and eat a meal. And *who* you eat with, remember, you become—just like you become *what* you eat:

> While they were eating, Jesus took the bread, blessed
> it, broke it, and then gave it to his disciples, saying,
> "Take and eat. *This is my body.*" And then he took a cup,
> blessed it, and gave it to his disciples, saying, "Drink
> from it, all of you. *This is my blood* of the covenant,
> which is being poured out for many for the forgiveness
> of sins. (Matt. 26:26–28)

Each Sunday, Christians come to a table ostensibly served with bread and juice, but in reality served with the body and blood of Christ.

Why?

Because eating is granting permission, and *what* you eat, you become. What you ingest, you unite with. You transform into—just ask Adam and Eve. Thus, by dining with Christ and ingesting Christ, Christians become Jesus to the world. Or as Paul says it, "Now *you* are the body of Christ" (1 Cor. 12:27 NIV, emphasis added).[2]

FROM UN-CREATION TO NEW CREATION
Granting God permission isn't a one-time affair. It's a daily discipline. A persistent struggle. A constant choice to dance with Life instead of death.

Many misunderstand transformation, expecting something more expedient. We envision the Holy Spirit's indwelling as a *moment* of complete and total transformation—going into the baptismal water only to come up no longer an addict, no longer an adulterer, no longer a liar, lunatic, or given to lust.

We view conversion as an end, instead of a beginning. The conclusion of *our* work and *God's* work, instead of where real work begins. We invite our neighbors to church, lead them to Christ, and then ignorantly hang a banner announcing "Mission Accomplished." The problem is: transformation isn't a *moment*; it's a *movement*.

Sure, testimonies of instantaneous transformation dazzle, but the allure is precisely because they are the exception. The "rule" is that transformation demands patience, process, a movement not imprisoned by a singular moment, but a weaving of infinite moments that guide us through turns and valleys like a stream enlarging into a raging river.

After conversion, Christians can still refuse to grant Jesus access, can still deny Jesus permission, can still ignore Christ's request to come in and eat a meal. Let's not forget, Judas sat at the Lord's Supper along with the other disciples, but when he took the bread from Jesus's hand, "Satan went into him" (John 13:26–27). Thus, claiming to be a follower of Jesus, going to church and small groups doesn't secure transformation. We *choose* who we become by the actions we embrace, by the permissions we grant, by the unions we pursue. And over time, and subtly so, we become who we choose to dine with, what we choose to ingest.

In other words, permission must be granted. *Daily.*

When we choose Christ, we surrender to a new way of living. We commit to learn a new language. We submit to a new way of thinking, a new way of acting, a new way of hoping, a new way of approaching death and living life. When we choose Christ, we become someone totally different. We are disciplined in love, infused with grace, and estranged from violence.

But this doesn't happen in a moment. It happens gradually. Slowly, with every choice, every day. So that over time, permission granted to God swells into a movement where sin is but a memory and death is no longer present at the dance.

CHAPTER TWELVE

Wishing Away the Day
The Transformation of Time

What was the serpent's tool of temptation in Genesis 3? Was it power? Was it arrogance? What deception did Satan wield to cause humanity to reach for the fruit? Was it greed? Lust?

It must've been powerful. Frighteningly so.

For Adam and Eve had everything—God's image (Gen. 1:26–27), God's blessing (Gen. 1:28), God's attention (Gen. 2:15–22), God's provision (Gen. 2:8–9), even complete sovereignty "over the fish in the sea and over the birds in the sky and over every living creature that moves on the earth" (Gen. 1:28), not to mention every plant and tree (Gen. 1:29). The serpent's tool of temptation, then, must possess immeasurable power. Terrifying potency, only matched by its subtlety.

An early church father named Irenaeus offered an answer often overlooked.[1] Irenaeus argued that Adam and Eve's sin wasn't arrogance or gluttony or lust or greed. But haste.[2] The serpent deceived them with haste. Humanity fell prey to haste.

I find it intriguing that God doesn't say in Genesis 1, 2, or 3 that humanity was *never* to eat of the tree of knowledge of good and evil—but he definitely says *not now* (Gen. 2:16–17; 3:1–3). If you eat from it *now*, the results will be disastrous. You can't handle it.

Later? Maybe. Now? Absolutely not.

Rules in our family follow the same logic. As soon as my oldest son, Zion, began to talk we had to outlaw the word "stupid." He'd throw this word around so carelessly we were afraid of his heart's ability to handle it. Not all words weigh the same, and this one was pretty hefty for a little guy only a couple of years into walking. So we outlawed the word. Forbade it. Told him, "Do *not* say that word."

Zion understood the boundary—a bit too well. He suddenly transformed into the "stupid" police, verbally embarrassing anyone who said it: "We don't say that word. That's a *baaaaaad* word. You can't say that word! Dad, they said the 's' word!"

After emotionally scarring the fourth college student with this shame tactic, I sat Zion down and explained: "Son, let me be more clear about our rule: *You* can't say the word 'stupid.' *Other* people can."

This simply didn't compute in my rule-following, cautious firstborn. So I made another run at it: "It's like this, buddy. Do Mommy and Daddy let you play with knives?"

He shook his head with furrowed brow.

"No," I continued, "because they're sharp and they could hurt you. But one day, you'll be old enough where you'll be able to use a knife without hurting yourself and without Mommy and Daddy's permission. It's just right now, you can't handle a knife. It could hurt you or you could hurt other people with it. But one day, you'll be able to handle it."

He nodded.

So I continued: "Words are the same way, buddy. They're sharp, powerful. And there are just some words that you're not ready to handle yet. Like the word 'stupid.' But one day, when you're older, you'll know exactly how to use words like 'stupid' in a way that doesn't hurt you or anyone around you. But that day *isn't* today."

I think God's command in Genesis 2 is the same. It's not that Adam and Eve could never eat from the tree, but *not* today. They just couldn't handle it. And God knew it. So he forbade it.

But the serpent's forked tongue stoked humanity's curiosity, ignited humanity's desire, and cajoled humanity to *haste*. Skipping steps in maturation. Skipping levels of progression. Taking a shortcut that gets us what we want, when we want it. And we want it now.

Eden's temptation, as sly as the serpent, indeed, was haste.

THE FRUIT OF HASTE

Haste is enticing. Intoxicating. To be able to acquire the treasure without any of the work, and to get it right now?

Hard to pass up.

But what haste doesn't tell you is the consequences of skipping steps. Of progressing too quickly. Of growing too much, too quick. In fact, that's the very definition of cancer. We all have cancer cells in us, and they aren't a problem. The problem is when they start to grow too fast, when they start to grow too much, too quick. A reality all too familiar, this hasty overproduction of cancer cells can kill us.

And haste is no different.

Haste is laced with violence. Violence against *time*—raging against the process, longing for the end, grasping for the goal without any of the steps in between. This was Satan's temptation of Jesus in the wilderness: "You want to establish a kingdom, Son of Man? I can give it all to you. *Without* the cross. We can skip that step altogether. All you need to do is bow down and worship me" (Matt. 4:8–9).[3]

This is the grammar of death. The language of the enemy. Impatience. Haste. Violence against time.

Haste seizes the fruit of Eden and assails the fruit of the Spirit. Peace is not possible when you live a life of haste. Haste is rarely gentle or kind, for, traditionally, immediacy demands a zeal forceful enough to break laws, to break our word, to act unfaithful. Haste doesn't produce goodness or love, even as it attempts to seize both. For haste violently and uncontrollably demands more and more, refusing to have its thirst quenched by the Living Water. Joy fades into the distance in haste's presence, for accepting the here and now is no longer possible since haste lusts for the future.

Haste rejects the image of God. For in God, there is no haste. God is patient. God is kind. God does not seize; he woos. God does not rush; he Sabbaths. God doesn't compromise his promises or overpower the will of others. No. God is steadfast. Faithful. His love *endures* forever. He pursues in the face of constant rejection, refusing to seize his treasure: *us*. Instead, like a loving father, he waits for us to return to him so that he can throw a party for his wayward child now home. Our God knows not haste, even in the presence of our rebellion. Just ask Hosea. Just ask Israel.

It's no wonder the fruit of the Spirit in Galatians 5 ends with "self-control" (the Achilles' heel of haste) and lists "patience" fourth—which we should probably translate as "un-haste." For the serpent subtly inserts haste into humanity's heart, slowly consuming us with each bite of fruit.

Haste: the ancient enemy of time. The ancient enemy of transformation.

The Burden of a Birthday

It's disorienting when someone makes you feel guilty for something you can't control.

No, I'm not talking about flatulence, being a "close talker," or being a jerk—for I believe there are avenues to address each of these issues and many others like them. I'm talking about something more innate. Something impossible to control. Something impossible to conceal.

I'm talking about growing up. Getting *older*.

The guilt-ridden comments usually come in cheerful tones, which sow seeds of distrust in little minds ("You sound cheery," ponders the child, "but why do I feel like I'm getting backhanded?"). The comments are usually something to the effect of, "Whoa! You're getting *so* tall! You stop getting older, now, you hear me" (ha, ha, ha . . . ho, ho, ho—[reaching toward the little one with a tousle of the hair]).

It's a strange encounter and a puzzling request: cease aging.

Of course, there's the more awkward version: "Oh my goodness, how old are you now? Well, if you're that old, then how . . . old . . . am *I*?" (ha . . . ha—[oh no]).

I mean, honestly, how do you respond to that? That moment where your mere existence causes another person to spiral into an existential crisis about their impending death.

Stop getting *older*?

Why can't growing up be celebrated instead of mourned? Why isn't someone's maturation greeted with excitement instead of the revving of the hearse's engine?

It's funny how getting older is met with surprise anyway—as if no one has mentioned this dirty little secret to us in our teens and twenties and we just *happen* upon it for the first time in our thirties, forties, and fifties through the growth of our children, grandchildren, or the medicine cabinet that expands with our age.

Stop getting *older*?

Sooner or later, we must accept that we can't run from our mortality. It seizes us regardless of our struggle. We all meet its gaze from time to time—for that's the price paid for "union" with death. It abrasively turns our face toward its gait in the presence of others or as we lie awake watching the clock tick ever forward.

It can't be ignored. It *will* be acknowledged. And not just on a deathbed.

TIME: THE TALE OF A TYRANT

When we engage getting *older* with fear and trembling, we transform *time* into a murderous adversary. *Time* becomes the unfair emperor who demands unfair taxation. *Time* the perpetrator of endless anxiety, tick-tocking away moments of our life and mutating them into measurements of our death. "Oh, *Time*, you cruel tyrant! Why do you rule with such an iron fist?!?!"

It's no wonder that a central part of Greek mythology was the exhile of Chronos, the Greek word for *Time*. The gods of Olympus seized Chronos and imprisoned him in Tartarus so they could reign without threat of mortality—sovereign rule without the threat of *Time*. Like most myths, this tale is a reflection of our desires, our pursuits, our issues.

Sure, today it's easy as adults to look at such stories, turn up our nose, and announce, "Thank God we aren't chained to such silly thinking anymore!" (Ha, ha, ha . . . ho, ho, ho—[with a smile fitting for foolish arrogance].) Yet we spend exorbitant amounts of money on anti-aging cream, Botox, and, if things really get bad, an entire face-lift. Billions of dollars spent trying to imprison Chronos. Trying to execute *Time*.

Youth is our definition of beauty because we loathe *time*. Hate *time*. Try to outrun *time*—a pursuit many of us continue after converting to Christianity: we worship Jesus because he's our nuclear weapon in our war on *time*. In him, we have the promise of eternal life—*time* without end. In him, we have the promise of heaven—where Chronos is expelled forever. In him, *time* is eventually damned to the lake of fire. One day, when we live in the sky, by-and-by.

With Jesus in hand, we taunt *time*, pretending it doesn't affect us at all—a façade commonly found at Christian funerals where everyone refuses to mourn. Refuses to weep. A luxury, ironically, not afforded to Jesus at the funeral for Lazarus where, standing at the tomb of his friend, "Jesus wept" (John 11:35).

We ignore *time* because we hate it. We wish *time* away because we don't understand it. We avoid *time*, berate *time*, vilify *time*, sacrifice *time* at the altar of haste, because, ironically, we're still addicted to the grammar of death. Still speaking the serpent's native tongue.

You see, *time* is defined by who our master is.

Or, to say it another way, *time* is defined by our chosen "union."

In our "union" with death, *time* is a measurement of decay. *Time* gauges the breakdown of our bodies as we draw closer to our master: death. For death is destructive—non-life, inanimate, deterioration. With death as our master, *time* is a measurement of decay. A measurement of our "union" with death.

If, though, we become one flesh with God through Christ, the Spirit transforms *time* from a measurement of decay into a measurement of re-union, redemption, re-creation into the image of God. In Christ, *time* no longer measures decline into death, but ascension into God. In Christ, *time* is no longer defined by the Fall, but by our holiness begotten in the womb of the Spirit living in us. In Christ, *time* becomes a measurement of our resurrection. Of our union with God.

Time is defined by our master, defined by our "end," defined by our union. So, in Christ, God *is time*.

The Liberation of Time

God is not "outside of time"; God *is time*. God is not constrained by time, nor is he disconnected from time. As the One "who is and who was and who is to come" (Rev. 1:4 NIV), God doesn't just *exist* in the past, present, and future, he *is* the past, present, and future. God is "the Alpha and the Omega, the Beginning and the End" (Rev. 21:6 NIV). God *is time*.

This doesn't mean all *time* is predestined, as if God's sovereign will tyrannizes time like death. No. God-*is-time* affirms his union with all of creation, realized in the incarnation and redeemed in the empty tomb. Christ ascends and the Spirit intends to transform all, redeem all, redefine all in him—even *time* itself. *Time* is not obliterated in God; *time* unites with God, interpenetrates with the eternal One.

Thus, our war with *time* is actually a war with God. A war with union. A war with transformation. A perilous embrace of haste.

Haste consumes us, oddly enough, ever so patiently. We often don't realize haste's presence until we're in a shouting match with our spouse over something as trivial as how to dispense the toothpaste. Haste works its way into our thoughts and actions like yeast into the dough, invading every space with no awareness of restraint or intention of stopping.

Haste resembles gluttony or lust or greed—sins with ravenous appetites and bottomless stomachs—yet appears much less grotesque. Haste is present in a newborn's cry for food that can't come quick enough or a diaper change that can't come fast enough. Haste lurks in the toddler's tender muse, "When I grow up, I'm gonna be a [fill in the blank]." Haste is found in the frustration of a preteen who doesn't have enough money to buy a hoverboard after mowing one lawn.

And like our desire for transformation, we never *outgrow* haste. As we become adults, it just changes form. Haste demands; haste rages; haste assaults time like a mortal enemy to be conquered. Haste wishes away the journey to simply get to the end. But in order to embrace transformation, we must divorce ourselves from haste. In order to empty ourselves to become one flesh with God, we must dissolve our union with haste. For transformation takes time. *Kenosis* takes time, patience, hard work. And, yes, even more time.

The good news is: in Christ, God *is* time. Or as Jesus says in John 17:3, "Eternal life [endless *time*] is to know God." An endless union with the infinite God throughout time eternal.

In Christ, time becomes a new wineskin ready to receive the outpouring of the divine in a union celebrated between the vessel and its contents. A new wineskin with no room for haste. Just more "time."

TRANSFORMING HASTE

My family and I host a community garden in our yard, and it's taught me a lot about God. The first Saturday, before we acquired an electric tiller, five to seven of us approached the ground with weapons of war: shovels, hoes, the works. I was assigned a six-foot by twelve-foot section to clear of rocks and till with a shovel— turning the soil over and over to purge it of impurities and prepare it to receive seeds. To receive life.

But first, I encountered the curse.

I could tell the ground wanted to produce life-giving fruit, but it fought me with a supernatural force. Hours later, however, mounds of rocks, a sore back, and several blisters demonstrated progress—albeit progress through pain.

We then placed new soil on top of the old, before acquiring several bags of compost to blanket the earth. For those with a black thumb, compost is nutrient-rich soil produced through the decomposition of animals, plants, cardboard, banana peels, and a lot of other decaying components. Yes, compost is a mess of death. Yet, in God's economy, death can be repurposed to bring life. Rich, nutrient-filled life, so that when seeds are planted within it, like a body placed in a tomb, a new birth occurs in the form of sprouts that eventually blossom into tomato plants, corn stalks, and melons. At the end of the day, we marveled at the conversion of our yard.

Gardening is immersed in transformation. And it has very little to do with haste. For one day doesn't produce fruit. It takes time.

The next phase was abhorrent, boring beyond compare. It was an excruciating combination of watering and waiting. Watering and waiting. Watering and waiting. Watering and . . . After several days, I actually stopped checking for fruit and just committed to the process of watering and ignoring. Watering and ignoring.

One day, though, our neighbor sent a text, filling my screen with a mound of dirt and a tiny greenish-yellow stalk piercing the ground. I couldn't believe it.

"When did that happen?"

I was conflicted with a mixture of "We did it!" and "I don't feel like we did anything."

It almost felt mysterious, somewhat divine—and definitely invigorating.

The next couple of days witnessed sprout after sprout, followed by length and height and volume and pride—deep, *deep* pride. Protective pride. Pride normally reserved for a parent and their child.

One day, I was sitting at our table, marveling at the rows of my "new children," when in my periphery sauntered a cautious yet determined rabbit—hopping and waiting, hopping and waiting, hopping and heading straight for our garden. I shot out the back door hissing (of all things!), gnashing my teeth (God, help me) at the wretched rabbit—who probably would've run away just as fast without all my theatrics.

"Great," I yelled, "*another* problem: How in the world do we keep these despicable vermin out of our garden?"

Research, more research; digging, more building. Fences, blockades. Boards, carefully placed rocks. The whole season we fought animal after animal. If it wasn't rabbits, it was groundhogs. If it wasn't groundhogs, it was raccoons. If it wasn't raccoons, it was some undetectable worm thing, or bug, or caterpillar of some sort, only admitting its presence through holes chewed in leaves. Even when we got most of this under control, some plants grew just fine but still produced rotten fruit. *Bad* fruit. For no reason that we could detect.

All of these trials, all of the frustration, all of the pain poured into our garden did, however, have a positive effect: We *savored* the good fruit. We gazed on the good fruit, recognizing its unique preciousness and value too often diminished by the mounds of produce at the grocery store. We delighted in each bite, as if the juice running down our chins was a libation in honor of a hard-fought victory.

You see, to garden, you must be willing to dig; you must be willing to endure pain. You must repurpose death, creatively fend off enemies, submit to the mystery of growth, and, yes, you must eradicate haste.

But this isn't just gardening. This is transformation.

CHAPTER THIRTEEN

THE PLACE OF PAIN

I'm not a runner. *At all.* In fact, I hate running, especially when it involves a track. No matter how hard I run, how fast I get my legs pumping, how much strain I exert or energy I expend, I end up in the same dang place. It's frustrating. Not that I have the endurance to go very far anyhow. Especially that first run after nine months of sedentary living. I have no idea what compels me to even break such an impressive streak of sitting. I don't know, maybe I should blame the summer Olympics for this sudden naïve inspiration (They just make it look so freaking easy). Without thinking, I put on my cutoff T-shirt, my baggy 1990s basketball shorts (I've never enjoyed the loincloth-type shorts most "serious" runners wear), and tighten my high-tops, only to stare down the vacant track thinking, "What in the *world* am I doing?"

Then, I'm off.

Steps four, five, and six send a surge of endorphins that makes me think, "*Okay.* All right. *That's* it—feel the release; embrace the energy."

It's at this point that foolishness takes over and I decide to increase the pace. "This is *easy.* I *got this.*" Rounding the first turn, reality starts to unsettle me: "Wait, I have to go around this track *how* many times for a mile?"

Suddenly things start to unravel: "Ouch, *yo* . . . what's that little pain in my side? Oh jeez, what did I eat this morning? Uh, I can still taste it—wait, am *I* about to throw up? Why won't this pain in my side go away? Actually I think it's getting worse—oh no. Oh *my* . . . my lungs are *burning* . . . why am I wheezing?"

The next thing I know, my Olympic dreams are shattered within the first lap, and the realization sets in: I have no endurance. I have very little patience. Especially in the face of pain.

WHERE TO BEGIN . . .

Alcoholics Anonymous got it right: the first step to transformation is admitting I have a problem. Admitting that something is lacking, that something needs to change. Admitting that I have a problem I can't solve by myself.

This first step is laced with pain. Overwhelming, gut-clenching pain, so severe, many never step foot on the track to transformation. Admitting I have a problem takes incredible courage—an immense amount of humility, honesty, energy, and vulnerability. This step requires a great amount of toil and reflection, an immeasurable effort to push through mounds of guilt and shame just to utter the words: I have a problem. I can't do this alone. I need help.

We spend so much time trying to avoid our stories, forget our pasts, cover our imperfections, and run from our shameful nakedness that many of us forget we're still wearing fig leaves. Treating transformation as a lie, or a rumor more fit for fairy tales, many of us never engage this first step, opting instead to just try to avoid the pain.

And we avoid pain *at all costs*.

Which makes sense. We weren't made to feel pain. We weren't made to experience death. We were made to live forever. This explains why funerals are so awkward. We don't know where to look, whether or not to laugh; we're frustrated we aren't crying enough, embarrassed we can't find the right words, worried we aren't wearing enough black to convince others, and ourselves, that we actually loved the deceased.

Funerals are an array of disorienting feelings, foreign to everyday life and the natural rhythms of our heart. Why? Because we were made in the image of a God that never dies. And so our mortality rages, knowing that our substance is more akin to immortality.

Yet, due to our union with death, pain is now commonplace. Present in the mundane activities of eating, walking, sleeping, breathing. We're saturated in physical and nonphysical pain that ever sings: We Weren't Meant To Live This Way. We weren't made for "union" with death. We were made for union with Life. With God himself. Yet as he approaches, we run for cover, trying not to be detected. Trying to escape the Light for a dark cave. Or at least just somewhere to hide from his gaze.

So, between two trees, we toil. We struggle between our desire to transform and our obsession with avoiding pain. We try to pretend we don't have a problem, because we fear that what follows such an admission is more and more pain. And we have no idea what to do when confronted with pain.

THE PLACE OF PAIN

God whispers to us in our pleasures, speaks in our conscience,
but shouts in our pain: it is His megaphone to rouse a deaf world.[1]
—C. S. Lewis

C. S. Lewis is an evangelical favorite, until some of his beliefs don't agree with ours. Then, like the Bible, his words are cut and pasted to fit our boxes of theology, neatly packaged and ready to move to another location. His Chronicles of Narnia take us to adventures beyond our world that provide illuminating reflections on our own. Theology flows from image to image, and since coming from a pretend Lion, it seems less fierce—yet, upon further investigation, is quite ferocious. We champion the epic, ushering our children into the wardrobe to lose themselves in the modern allegory, that is until Emeth, the follower of the false god Tash, appears in the final book and is embraced by Aslan as one of his own, causing us to squirm a bit, having already attended Lewis's evangelical coronation.

In full disclosure, I'm guilty of this same *embrace*-wait-now-*repulsion* toward Lewis. For example, his quote above. Or at least the way in which people typically quote Lewis's observation of pain. First, let's consider the *embrace*.

It's true: "our pleasures" seem to mute God more than magnify him. We typically treat pleasure as our *end* instead of the *means* that can guide us back to our *true* end, God. If we so let them. Pleasures are arrows pointing heavenward. Yet generation after generation proves that instead of pleasures leading us deeper into God, they prevent us from reaching God.

Why? Because we don't know how to receive gifts.

We receive gifts selfishly and without true satisfaction—neither of which is a path to the crucified King who didn't consider equality with God something to be grasped. Thus, material "blessings" turn out to be a heap of hellish curses driving us further away from God instead of toward him. Not because pleasures are the problem. *We* are. We're the problem.

We look to pleasures to cure our problem of pain. But they can't deliver. They don't have the capacity. Instead, our embrace of pleasures creates a more troublesome problem: God's voice, ever the same volume, passes through pleasures muffled. Muted. Or, as Lewis states, as a "whisper."

God's voice increases decibels in our "conscience." Yet, as Lewis suggests, not as loud as one would assume. With our conscience, the problem, though, isn't typically the *volume* of God's voice. He simply struggles to get a word in edgewise.

There's a cacophony of other voices cluttering our conscience. For some, like myself, God's voice rivals the blaring voice of accusation constantly chattering in my soul. That accusing voice fills the space of my heart with negative noise, usually increasing in volume when other voices try to speak and shouting the loudest in moments of ethical decision. Others are plagued with a quiet, small, yet tyrannical voice—the voice that pierces a table conversation not because of its boorish nature, but because of its tender, soothing quality. The voice that, when it speaks, everyone stops to savor the rare occasion, intently waiting for whatever may come, always labeling the words as "wisdom" even if they're utterly foolish. Internally, God's voice struggles to be heard because so many other attendees have been invited to the party, chatter creating white noise mimicking a box fan.

In our conscience, God speaks. It's just really hard to hear him above the noise.

The Repulsion of Lewis's Quote

Lewis's quote climaxes, though, with the voice of God in pain, stating and restating pain's significance and God's volume: "*But [God] shouts in our pain: it is His megaphone to rouse a deaf world.*" Let me affirm this powerful statement, and then deny it.

It doesn't take long as a pastor to witness the transformative power of pain. Even the most hardened scoundrels reveal soft spots in their armor when tragedy strikes, when a diagnosis is pending, when pain takes up residence. Brokenness has a way of expanding our tightly packed hearts, revealing space for something else to be collected. Pain fertilizes the soil of our hearts with a willingness to listen, even if the sprouts of the message have yet to reveal a rose or a dandelion.

Yes, the opportunity for transformation in moments of pain is undeniable. Pain has a way of shattering our order, reminding us of our inability to control, sitting us down to "have a long talk." Pain presses conversations about our jobs ("What am I doing with my life?"), our priorities ("I'm tired of not seeing my family"), and even our mortality ("Would anyone miss me if I was gone?"). For pain is a rude reminder of a union from days gone by that we numb, run, and fake slumber in order to avoid. Pain reminds us of death. Our death. Our inevitable end that we can't prevent with any amount of money, opioids, or plastic surgeries. And when pain turns our face toward the menacing presence of its master, we can't help but search for its opposite: life. Or, should that word be capitalized?: Life.

I love that Jesus transforms the abstract into a person, incarnating what we cannot see, forcing us to capitalize words once thought generic. Jesus reveals:

"*I am* the Way, the Truth, and the Life." (John 14:6)

When we drown out the voice of God, we reposition Truth from a person to follow into an idea to be pondered, an object to be dissected, a thought to be dismissed. "But Truth," John 14:6 interjects, "is not an *object* but a *subject*, not an *idea* but a *person*." For Truth is Christ—and so is Life.

Life is not something we possess; it's the One who longs to be our possession. Jesus is Life, and can be found oftentimes sitting next to death. Not because he enjoys the company (although not as terrified as we, so I've heard), but because Jesus knows where humanity tends to look first. He knows what captures our gaze. He knows that since the first tree of life, we continually look toward death. To catch our eye, Jesus simply follows the trajectory of our gaze and takes a seat—next to death. Indeed, the volume of God's voice increases in pain because we turn our eyes and ears in his direction, intending to lock eyes with death only to find another visitor in Christ.

It's Lewis's last clause I reject—and I think he would as well—even though it's the portion most oft quoted with beatific delight: *"[Pain] is His megaphone to rouse a deaf world."* Or, as I first heard the quote, "[Pain] is [God's] megaphone." A metaphor's entire purpose is to grasp at what is beyond, to stretch words beyond themselves in order to catch a glimpse of the divine and bring it back into our world. Like Plato's instructive cave, metaphors use the shadows in our world to describe the true form in the world beyond: using the physical to describe what is nonphysical, the reflection to describe the reality. Thus, it's not surprising that metaphors about God fall apart when pressed too tightly—for even poetry can only stretch so far into the infinite. Now what is described is true, just muddied when it passes the veil from heaven to earth. And Lewis's metaphor struggles with the same limitations in this last phrase.

My primary contention is the possessive pronoun "His" and how people quoting Lewis often understand it. Pain is "God's" possession used as a tool, like a megaphone, to scream his messages toward humanity. Megaphones can be obnoxious, especially in the hands of someone with the maturity of a sixth grader. Sure, in some scenarios, a megaphone is a necessary tool among other tools: to instruct a crowd, to communicate with a ledge-jumper, or to control the unruly. As humans we understand this, but when applied to God it creates significant problems.

The possessive pronoun "His" suggests a dependence by God on pain. And when attached to the "megaphone" metaphor, pain is transformed into not just a tool among others, but the most effective tool at God's disposal to relay his messages to humanity. At which point, one must wonder, did God truly give Adam and Eve a chance at obedience if he didn't use his megaphone before the Fall? Lewis's metaphor begins to quiver under the weight of such inquiries, for at a certain point the megaphone reveals that God depends on pain, indeed *must have* pain, in order to effectively communicate with his prized creation. Thus good without evil is less than good, at least at communicating.

And that is simply *not* true. Good is *not* dependent on evil, but only the inverse. Good needs not evil to exist, but only the opposite. God doesn't need pain to speak to his creation, for love is quite adequate to accomplish the job.

Love ventures into places long forgotten or intentionally avoided, walking down seedy streets shining a brilliant light so that passersby won't step on the exposed needles lining the curb. Love knows no limits, is omnipresent, and refuses to be pushed out of any caveat or corner that darkness or pain tries to commandeer. If anything, love amplifies God's voice, for, as John reveals, "God *is* love" (1 John 4:16b).

And love doesn't mix well with pain.

Love never wields pain as a weapon or uses pain to increase its presence. In fact, pain shrouds the presence of love. Pain covers love and tries to completely conceal love's radiance, but is unsuccessful. For love has a way of piercing the darkest night, taming the greatest pain, and drowning out the grandest evil, even if it's wielding a megaphone.

Coming Alive

God doesn't cause pain. It's not a weapon he chooses. It's not a tool he depends on to communicate with his beloved creation. But in this world between two trees, where the presence of death pervades, pain is common. Especially on the path to transformation.

A friend of mine was a minister for thirty years. He had many gifts—great speaker, great exegete, great leader. But above all other gifts, he had an uncanny ability to meet people in their darkest moments and whisper just the right words to urge them deeper into their night of pain only to gently guide them to the light of Christ's new dawn.

He'd been working with a recovering meth addict for about six weeks—the man who now sat weeping next to my friend on the tailgate of his beat-up pickup truck. The man was sobbing almost uncontrollably. The pain was simply too much.

"I can't do this anymore," he said to my friend. "I just *can't* do this. I hurt all day . . . every single day . . . I hurt and hurt and HURT!" As his voice reached the level of a megaphone, the man let out a sigh of resignation: "At least when I was on meth I could still smile." Shaking his head, he whispered, "I can't do this anymore."

My friend nodded, wiped his nose with his hanky (as was his custom), exhaled deeply, and gently responded, "Johnny, have you ever fallen asleep on your arm? You know, you wake up in the middle of the night, having laid on your arm for two or three hours, cutting off all the blood to your limb so that when you touch it with your other hand, you feel nothing. Just a mushy mass that doesn't even feel like it's a part of your body?"

The addict nodded, a bit puzzled, but he definitely understood the scenario.

"I don't know about you," my friend continued, "but it kind of freaks me out a bit. So I start shaking and shaking my hand until all of a sudden it starts to tingle, but then, oh boy, *then* it starts to hurt. It hurts to touch something; it hurts to rest it on my leg; it hurts when I shake it and when I don't shake it. Yet slowly but surely, the blood fills the limb, and my arm comes back to life—moving about, once again useful, and free from pain."

Pausing for a moment, allowing his parable to linger in the air, my friend turned toward the man and said, "I'm so glad you're feeling pain. Because that tells me you're coming alive. The healing blood of Jesus is filling your body, and *you're coming alive.*"

In a world caught between two trees, pain is common. Especially on the path to transformation. Pain is the grammar of death. Pain is the native tongue of the enemy gifted to creation when we became one flesh with death. Yet when we find ourselves swallowed in agony's embrace, we can be confident that Life is soon to follow. That healing is on the horizon. That, in Christ, the cross always ends with an empty tomb.

TRAGEDY AND THE CHURCH

On May 22, 2011, a third of my hometown of Joplin, Missouri, was wiped out by an EF-5 tornado. The devastation and pain was massive. This rain-wrapped tornado stretched a mile wide with winds over two hundred miles an hour. For thirty-eight minutes, the disastrous winds traveled 22.1 miles on the ground, leveling over seven thousand homes and countless businesses, including the 15th Street Walmart and St. John's Hospital. The sheer power is impossible to describe—wooden boards pierced metal buildings, twigs embedded in curbs, and 158 lives were lost as the storm blew into a memory. Almost ten years later, the scars from the powerful winds are still visible in the land, although so too is healing. Healing that began moments after the funnel retreated.

Over the course of the next several months, a force more powerful than the tornado took action: the church. The body of Christ. The dwelling place of Life, Love, and Jesus. The unity among the eighty or so churches and twenty or so denominations was startling. In fact, the head of FEMA—when he wasn't busy arguing with the head of the Red Cross over who would get credit for the

St. Mary's Catholic School, Church, and Rectory on 23rd Street in Joplin, Missouri, after the EF-5 tornado on May 22, 2011, with only the cross still left standing. Photo courtesy of Gregg Murdock.

relief efforts—told a group of Christian leaders: "I've never seen anything like this. You guys really don't even need us with all of the churches coming together like this."

As difficult as the time was and as painful as the emotional and physical cleanup efforts have been, the aftermath of the tornado was a sweet time for the city of Joplin. Visitors from all over the country, all over the world, poured into our southwest Missouri home, giving us the gift of their efforts while we gave them the gift of the gospel. It was amazing. Each Sunday our church was graced with baptism after baptism as the cleanup efforts spread into the hearts and lives of those who thought they were there to serve us. Our pain became a beacon for the lost. Our rubble became fertile soil for the gospel.

In this world caught between two trees, God doesn't need pain to reach us, but he chooses to meet us *in it*. For healing. For transformation. For union. For as the storms of our lives settle, one thing remains: the tree of life. The cross of Calvary.

187

CHAPTER FOURTEEN

THE WONDER OF *WITH*

If I had to pick just one word to describe the Lord, it would be the word *with*.

With is a powerful term, substantially outperforming other prepositions. *With* communicates togetherness, intentional relation, the ministry of presence. *With* embodies the notion of a gift or an exchange of some sort, approaching relational self-giving or *kenosis*. Embedded in *with* is a movement toward.

It's quite unlike the word "from," which moves *away* from others, emphasizing something closer to self-serving or anti-*kenosis*: "the merchants of the earth grew rich *from* [the prostitute's] excessive luxuries" (Rev. 18:3 NIV). "From" siphons instead of infuses, takes instead of bestows, abandons instead of dwells *with*. "From" asks for something in return, whereas *with* asks for nothing at all. Just to be *with* someone is enough. Just presence—whether we're talking about pain or simply the mundane.

With moves toward, alongside of, in the presence of. *With* invigorates and enlivens in a manner much different than "near," yet carries the dignity and intensity of the word "among" or "at," each emphasizing a "shared presence"—something that "near" or "around" could never fully appreciate.

For instance, after a long trip—say driving from Rhode Island to Missouri in a twenty-five-hour car ride with four kids over a two-day period after a three-week stay—being "near" my house elicits a much different response than being "at" my house. Living "near" my family is a far cry from living *with* my family. *With* surpasses the "relative closeness" that constrains words like "near" or "around" or "almost." Instead, *with* stretches the limits of our space, pressing "closeness" to its breaking point into other areas beyond just the physical. Similar to the word *union*.

With is central to the heart of God, at the core of the gospel message. In fact, Matthew bookends his entire Gospel with the word. In Matthew 1, an angel of the Lord appears to Joseph to not only prevent him from following through with his plan to quietly divorce Mary, but also to reveal the divine identity of the child: "Behold, the virgin will conceive and give birth to a son, and they will call him Immanuel, which means 'God *with* us'" (Matt. 1:23). Matthew's Gospel begins announcing not God "near" us or "around" us, but Immanuel—God *with* us.

After Jesus's Sermon on the Mount (Matt. 5–7), his twelve-fold healing cluster (Matt. 8–9), the sending of the twelve disciples (Matt. 10), the transfiguration (Matt. 17), the crucifixion (Matt. 27), and the resurrection (Matt. 28:1–10), Matthew ends his Gospel the way it began. The very last words of his text, written in red letters, announces: "I [Jesus] am *with* you always—to the very end of the age" (Matt. 28:20 NIV, emphasis added).

Immanuel: God *with* us, Jesus *with* us, the Spirit *with*in us. Whether in a place of pain or a position of poverty, whether in an eruption of laughter or a depiction of joy, whether in the radical or the ordinary, God is _with_.

WITH THE WORD

It's easy to overlook the power of words, especially when they're as small as the word *with*. We use words so often and in so many different settings we forget how sharp they are. We handle them flippantly, tossing them around like spoons thrown into a drawer while emptying the dishwasher instead of like the steak knives they are. The frequency of our words, both internally and externally, causes us to take them for granted. To forget their explosiveness. To forget that with a single word, God called creation into existence. To forget that, in Christ, "The Word became flesh and made his dwelling among us" (John 1:14 NIV).

In social media posts, political debates, and even pulpits, words are used haphazardly. Irreverently. Forgetting the divine potency therein. Our impious attitude toward words even finds its way into childhood rhymes intended to pay forward wisdom but that instead sow seeds of folly: "Sticks and stones can break my bones, but words . . . [finish it]."

Yep, "but words can never hurt me."

That's stupid. That saying is absolutely absurd.

I remember coming home from preschool after a pretty exhausting half day filled with more conflict and tension than normal. Maybe I didn't sleep well the night before or maybe I was just in an irritating mood—I'm really not sure *why* what happened *happened*. All I know is things got kind of dicey at recess when another boy and I got into a bit of a tussle over the one-seater "Little Tikes" Cozy Coupe—you know, the Flintstone-esque plastic car fit with a steering wheel, two swinging doors, and the classic yellow roof. When all was said and done, *I* got the car but he got the final word: "You're a jerk!"

On the drive home, I sat quietly in my booster seat reflecting on the fact that, even though I got the toy, I felt like I'd lost something. My mom, noticing my demeanor, asked through the rearview mirror, "Is everything okay, honey?" After I filled her in on the playground combat, my mom assuaged my pain with the rhythmic "wisdom": sticks-and-stones-can-break-my-bones-but-words . . .

Words hurt. Words scar. Words cut so deep, I think I'd rather have you hit me with a stick or a stone. I mean, flesh wounds heal after a couple of days, but words linger. They loom. Reappear years later in a fleeting dream, a passing thought, or in the look of a loved one. Words wound in ways and places Band-Aids can't help—even if the bandage is decorated with my favorite superhero.

Words have power, and they should be treated with care.

Words have the power to start revolutions, end feuds, condemn the innocent, liberate the lonely, or shatter shame. Words can create and destroy. Words can heal and wound. Words can move us into and out of depression, off or onto a ledge, away from or toward love. Words are potent with power and should be treated as such.

It's not surprising, then, that Jesus is depicted in Revelation 19 as a victorious rider on a white horse, whose "name is the *Word* of God" (Rev. 19:13)—the same name given to Jesus to start John's Gospel: "In the beginning was the *Word*. The *Word* was *with* God, and the *Word* was God" (John 1:1). The Word of God calms the storm with whispered rebuke (Matt. 8:26b). The Word of God ushers Lazarus from the grave with the simple command "Come out" (John 11:43). The Word of God becomes flesh and dwells among us (John 1:14) to comfort the distressed ("Do not fear," Rev. 1:17), to compel the dispirited ("Be earnest and repent," Rev. 3:19), and to make everything new (Rev. 21:5). The Word of God comes with power to be *with*.

And the presence and power of the Word demands a response.

SANITY AND THE SABBATH

I struggle with Sabbath. Mightily. I struggle with just being *with* the Lord.

I have the blessed addiction to be either "all" or "nothing at all." Sure, this is celebrated when I am in the "all" mode, for people laud with envy, "Man, when you're focused, you're like . . . like . . ."

"Neurotic," I interject.

"*No*, like *locked-in*."

"No," I correct, "the word you're looking for is *in-sane*."

From time to time, I genuinely wonder about my sanity. It's something I actually fear—my mind betraying me; losing my ability to think, interact, remember. Whether it be dementia, Alzheimer's, or something totally undiagnosable, I fear my mind betraying me, although at times it feels like we were never really allies to begin with.

When my mind decides to take control, whether it be two in the afternoon while playing a game of Bohnanza with the family or two in the morning when I just woke up to go to the bathroom, my mind can ignite and send me into an internal battle between my desire for peace and my urge to solve all my problems and the problems of everyone around me, albeit through the lens of exaggerated delirium. In those moments, I feel a further tear in the fabric of my soul—a tear that ever increases along a fragile seam that, if exhausted, will rend my very ability to be sane. I have a friend who tells me (quite often, come to think of it) that he envisions me as an old man, sitting in a chair in a nursing home, muttering incoherently to myself various fragments of conspiracy theories with drool coming out one side of my mouth and in the corner of the other side remnants from yesterday's lunch (little does he know I simply call this Saturday night when Sara and the kids are out of town). Not sure if he's a prophet or the son of a prophet (although he works for a nonprofit), but the struggle is real and the scenario isn't as far-fetched as I would hope.

My struggle with sanity directly correlates to my struggle with Sabbath. You know, Sabbath: one of the Ten Commandments we ignore with more frequency than "thou shalt not murder" or "thou shalt not commit adultery," which given our culture's obsession with war and sex, is saying something.

We mock Sabbath. We worship workaholism. We laugh in the face of rest as if it were a naïve child foolishly asking for ice cream at dinner. America's damning adage "More is better," while rarely said, is embedded in the passive-aggressive comments of colleagues and the bloated job descriptions that fit on a single sheet of paper yet contain four full-time positions (usually concealed in the line "And other tasks assigned at the discretion of the supervisor"). The schedule demands more hours than we care to offer, the people demand more interaction than an introvert should be required to surrender, and Sabbath is as rare as a pearl in the mouth of an oyster at a Red Lobster. We neglect Sabbath, are addicted to busyness, and ingest task after task as our drug.

THE DARK NIGHT OF *WITH*

A couple of summers ago, the Lord took me to a dark place to refashion my soul. I had just finished a ten-year sprint filled with marriage, four children, one miscarriage, five new homes (including a spell of living overseas), eight years of housing people in need, loads of traveling and speaking, the completion of five degrees, two books, and three full-time ministries. For years my community had been challenging me to simplify my schedule, and while I'd taken steps, the chaos was still raging. But finally everything was coming together, and *finally* my schedule was starting to settle down.

At the time, I didn't have another commitment on my schedule for eight weeks—eight solid weeks with no projects due, no books to write, papers to turn in, sermons to preach, conferences to attend. Eight weeks of space for the Lord to dig deep in my soul and move me toward transformation.

And *it was painful*. Excruciatingly painful. At times, simply unbearable.

During this "dark night of the soul," I genuinely felt like I was dying. I couldn't sleep; I was overcome with fear, with patience, with anxiety, with love for my family. I was so overwhelmed that I even asked my wife not to sleep on her side with her back to me, but to hold my hand as we fell asleep so that I could be close to her. As an introvert who's never been real touchy-feely, this was quite a request.

Of course, everyone had a diagnosis for me: midlife crisis, depression, anxiety, the ever-present "he finally went nuts." But I knew it was something different. A repositioning of the tectonic plates of my soul by the Spirit to position me toward a new work, a new way forward, a new identity. Toward the God of *with*.

Throughout the sleepless nights and blurry days, the Lord had a persistent but clear message to me. One that shocked me. Not because of its profundity but because of its simplicity:

"Shane, you are really good at doing things *for* me, but you are terrible at doing things *with* me."

At first, it was hard for me to hear and even more difficult to understand. Initially, I thought he was disappointed in my work. I thought my offerings to him were being rejected, and, in some ways, I boiled with the frustration of Cain.

"After all I've done, after all I've given up for you, it's still not enough? You're still dissatisfied with my offering? Was it the hours? Sixty to seventy a week isn't enough for you? What, the quality wasn't up to your standard? It wasn't perfect enough for you?"

I raged. Frustrated and angry with the Lord and his audacity to critique my gifts to him. And for a while, I quit talking to him altogether.

But the Spirit tenderly led me to understand God's heart in this revelation of *with*: it's not the "product" he's confronting, but the "process" of my work. My ignorance of his presence in my work. My avoidance of his presence almost altogether. My rejection of the gift of *with*.

Although I hadn't realized it, the last ten years I'd been working frantically to try to convince myself that I was valuable to the Lord. I would often say (whether out loud or in the reel in my head), "I just want him to say, 'Job well done, good and faithful servant.' That's it. That's all I want from him." Often our relationship would look something like me sitting at a desk for hours on end, finishing my work, and then going to the location where I "kept" the Lord to ask: "Do you like it? Do you like my work? I made it for you. Will you bless it?"

What I failed to understand was that I was selling the goal short. My target was too small. God was pleased with the "things" I was doing—that wasn't the issue. What was motivating his upheaval of me was not displeasure, but his desire to be *with* me.

You see, the true blessing of the work wasn't in the quality or effectiveness of the product but in the process of producing the work *with* the Lord.

"Shane, stop doing things *for* me, and start doing things *with* me. Work *with* me. Sabbath *with* me. Just be *with* me."

I'm not sure why this surprised me, given that God's name revealed to Moses at the burning bush is "I AM" (Exod. 3:14), which literally means "to be." "To be" present. "To be" *with*. It hit me hard: if I'm going to connect *with* God (the great "I AM"), then I must make an intentional shift from "doing" to "being"—from doing things *for* God to being *with* God.

Busyness is our cancer that resists the chemo of Sabbath. That wars against *with*. Busyness deceives us like a serpent, filling five days a week with frenzy and then still seeping into the cracks of our Sabbath. Saturday morning, instead of sleeping in, the subconscious is filled with topics like yesterday's meeting or Thursday's evaluation or last Tuesday's vicious email. By the time these anxieties begin to fade, it's Sunday afternoon, and the rest of the day is spent wrestling with the rapidly approaching presence of Monday. Bloody Monday.

The seven-day cycle wars against Sabbath. Presses us with a pace that has no space for *with*. Convinces us that the more we do, the more we're worth and the more we're accepted. Which is simply not true.

NEVER ALONE

The power of *with* is felt in its inversion: "alone."

Taking a break from writing, my daughter and I left the office, meandering through the downtown streets of Providence, Rhode Island. We've traveled a lot this summer, and we're ten days into this twenty-one day trip purposed to create some space for me to write.

My daughter is a deep well who feels so intensely that her emotions arise only to bottleneck near the surface, causing confusion in her heart. We talk often about this gift and the difficulty that comes with it. She is steadily understanding that the best approach is to fumble through words and sift through the wreckage of the rubble in her heart to unearth the true source of her emotion, whether positive or negative.

Yesterday, through tears, she told me she wanted to go home. I was proud of her. Proud of her for speaking up, for allowing the emotions to take shape in words that expressed the depths of her heart. Today, as we walked the city streets, I asked her again how she was doing. She smiled as we traversed the crosswalk hand in hand: "I'm okay—I still miss home."

I nodded in understanding. "Okay, well, when are your best moments here? What moments make you feel the most alive and at peace here?"

Without hesitation she said, "When I'm *with* you or Mom one-on-one."

As we crossed the street, I asked, "Is that why you wanted to come to work *with* me this afternoon?"

She nodded her head in affirmation.

"Okay," I paused, "when are your worst moments here?"

She thought for a moment, giving her answer careful attention. Finally, she said, "When you're at work and Mom is helping with the little kids and the boys are playing video games."

"Why are those the worst moments? I mean, you're *with* people, right?"

"Yeah," she responded, "but even when I'm around other people I can still feel alone."

I love being a dad. I learn something new about the Lord every day through my children's struggles, their successes, their maturation (or lack thereof), and their piercing insights like this one. This revelation of presence. Of the power of *with*. Of the potency of the Word that became flesh to dwell *with* us. Not around us, not ignoring us, not merely moving across the street yet hidden by shrubbery and a garage door. But *with* us.

My daughter taught me the key to the Lord's message. For years, I've worked *for* the Lord, in his presence but never acknowledging him. Engaging him. Resting in him. Working "around" him, but not *with* him. Yet blaming him when I felt alone. In pain. Confused and wandering.

Hand in hand with my daughter, it struck me: transformation is a discipline of embracing the Word *with*. *With* convicts, comforts, compels, corrects, emboldens; it creates gratitude, clarity, courage, and intimacy. *With* invites community, purpose, productivity, vulnerability, and Sabbath. *With* counters isolation, calms the storms in our lives, and offers a calling without end. *With* is holy, divine, and carries a potency too often overlooked and underappreciated.

If union with death leads to isolation, union with God leads to the preposition *with*. For wounds begin to heal in the presence of *with*. Pain becomes bearable in the presence of *with*. Addictions lose their grip, division fades away, the ordinary becomes divine, and death becomes a stranger in the power and presence of *with*.

For his name is Immanuel, God *with* us, calling us *to be with* him.

CHAPTER FIFTEEN

TRUE HUMANITY
The Redemption of Christian Works

Between two trees, on the path of transformation, where do *works* fit? What place do *works* hold in our relationship with God? Works of service, works of compassion, works of sacrifice—what do we do with *works*?

Protestants struggle with works, at times treating them like a life-threatening allergy or a four-letter word instead of five. We know works belong, and all Christians should be encouraged to do them, but works are only awkwardly embraced—invited to the party only because Mom made us, but then exiled to the outskirts of the room. Yet we are confident works have a place in the church, even enlisting shame and guilt, whether in the pulpit or in casual conversation, to compel other Christians to *do works*—a passive-aggressive church culture policed by unknown agents through snide remarks, disapproving looks, and petty passing comments flaunting busy schedules filled with nursery duty, Sunday school lessons, and potlucks where we cook the most, eat the least, and always fight to go last in line, but are ever quick to point out, "Works don't save us!"

We say this too often, and, to be honest, we do so with an edge of insecurity. "I do works, preacher, *but not to get to heaven*. For there is only one work by which I am saved [flashing the happy plastic smile with Bible in tow]." Every church "work" day, every volunteer monologue, every preacher Jesus-juke eventually gets around to *demanding* works and simultaneously *debasing* them as "unimportant for salvation," or, at the very least, not *essential*.

Martin Luther was so paranoid about works that he advocated the dismissal of James and the book of Revelation from the Bible, concluding about Revelation: "Christ is neither taught nor known in it."[1] Indeed, if you are championing "faith *alone*," passages like these are more than troublesome.

> What good is it, my brothers and sisters, if someone claims to have faith but has no deeds? Can such faith save them? . . . [for] faith alone, if not accompanied by works, is dead. (James 2:14, 17)

> Behold, I am coming soon, and my reward is with me. I will repay each person according to what they have done. (Rev. 22:12)

If works have no place, then passages like these are considered a betrayal. A distorted gospel, where deeds have too great a role in discussions of salvation. Yet the New Testament is clear: works matter.[2] Works are *not* disregarded because of the cross. Works have a significant role in the Christian life, and the New Testament uncompromisingly demands we do them. Which is a difficult truth to accept for both the reformers and the perfectionists among us.

The God of the Perfectionist

There are passages of Scripture that genuinely make me tremble at their call. At times confronting and at times compelling, the Word of God responds to my invitation of intimacy, and sometimes it's simply overwhelming. For instance, as I flip happily to the Sermon on the Mount, a pall passes over me as I remember the beautiful beatitudes begin a chapter that ends with the ghastly "Therefore, be perfect, as your heavenly Father is perfect" (Matt. 5:48). As a perfectionist with a tendency toward legalism, the only other passage in red letters I fear more is:

> Many will say to me on that day, "Lord, Lord, did we not prophesy in your name and in your name drive out demons and in your name perform many miracles?" Then I will declare to them, "I never knew you. Away from me, you evildoers!" (Matt. 7:22–23)

These texts ignite my anxiety, confident I don't measure up. I lash myself for flaws, inherent or acquired. I beat my flesh, hoping for submission, only to produce more rebellion. In my mind, I am the judge, jury, and prosecutor of my own soul, and I'm always found guilty of one thing: imperfection.

Grace rarely finds a home in my heart, and peace is a stranger passing in the crowd.

Perfectionism haunts me when I'm awake and even when I'm asleep. For years I've been tormented by the same recurring dream: a large home, dark and old inside, clearly located in a shady part of town. My family is asleep, relying on me to lock up and keep us safe. I go from door to door, latching each deadbolt and hanging each chain, when through the curtain I catch a glimpse of a moving shadow. Quickly I mentally inventory each door, remembering two in the back yet to be locked and, of course, in the exact location toward which the shadows were moving. I dart past the antique-furniture-obstacle-course, successfully securing the first door only to arrive at the second door to find the lock faulty. I turn the deadbolt in vain, panicking further with each unsuccessful latch. The dream never ends with the shadowy figures bursting through the door, but I wake up with two quite familiar emotions:

anxiety (not knowing where or when the attack will come) and shame (for once again, I've failed). Two emotions that for years have characterized my interaction with God—anxiety that no matter how hard I work he will still find the vulnerable spot in my case for heaven and so, in shame, I approach him knowing that I've failed, that I've "fallen short of the glory of God" (Rom. 3:23).

The dream taunts my subconscious and surfaces with the conscious reminder that I'm not perfect like my heavenly Father is perfect. Or, as Peter (of all people) puts it, I'm not "holy as [my heavenly Father] is holy" (1 Pet. 1:16). I'm unholy. I'm imperfect. And I fear there's no hope of ever being different.

It's no wonder Christians move along a spectrum of being judgmental or hypocritical, because, let's be honest, Scripture sets the standard pretty high and the majority of us simply crack under the pressure. No amount of effort seems enough. No amount of praying proves sufficient. No amount of accountability partners, Bible studies, devotions, small groups, service projects, mission trips, sermons, services, conventions, or WWJD bracelets seem to work. Because the more I strain for perfection, the more I find myself in the same damn place—or worse off than I was before.

I mean, there are endless reasons to feel guilty in the church— mounds of evidence proving my imperfection. It feels like every sermon I'm reminded of something I'm not doing very well. In fact, recently I wondered aloud on social media: "In the Evangelical church have we lost the ability to use any other tactic besides guilt? #shameisntenough" What startled me was the response: hundreds of likes, dozens of comments, and not one of them negative. All in agreement that Christians are carrying burdens of perfectionism that mock Matthew 11:28–30:

> Come to me, all who are weary and burdened, and I
> will give you rest. Carry my yoke upon you and learn

from me. For I am gentle and humble in heart, and you will find rest for your souls. For my yoke is easy and my burden is light.

I'd never call Jesus a liar (I'm too obsessed with divine holiness for that), but at times this verse tempts me to cross that line. For the call to perfection, to the same holiness as God is simply exhausting. A burden I'd never refer to as "light."

And so, not knowing where *works* fit, many Christians become addicted to pain, thinking, "If it doesn't hurt, then I must be doing something wrong." So, instead of God, we begin to search for struggle, search for crisis. We latch on to books like *Radical*, heaping shame on our narrative because grace just isn't enough. We transform faithfulness into rejecting the routine, bypassing the ordinary, and looking for crisis to remind us that by *our* wounds we are healed. And yet, the result is just a spiral of wandering, never belonging, always searching for our newly fashioned God: pain.

WHEN SIN BECOMES A WAY OF LIFE

Yet I loathe the other extreme in the church just as much. Typically found in evangelical circles, the "seeker sensitive" strand essentially rips Matthew 5:48 and 1 Peter 1:16 out of the Bible. And they flaunt it. In announcements, in Communion meditations, in sermons, in altar calls, in calls to worship, in closing songs, in the bulletin, on T-shirts, on bracelets, on stickers fixed to either the back window of their vehicles or brazenly placed on the cover of their Holy Bibles, a singular message resounds:

> "Hey, man, it's cool. *We're all sinners.* Even though I'm the preacher, I'm just like you. I'm not holier than you or more perfect than you. *I'm just a sinner like everybody else.*"

205

Well, that's depressing. I mean, I know what they're *trying* to do, but in their attempt at relatability all they've actually said is:

> "Even though I've been doing this Christian thing for
> more years than you've been alive and even though I'm
> a freak about it, nothing about me has really changed.
> I'm still just like I was when I started! Not holier. Not
> more perfect. Just a sinner like you!"

[handwritten margin note: I do this in speaking. Point is to try and God's way on grace.]

Maybe it's just me, but I don't find this comforting at all. In fact, I find it appalling. Because the only solace I find in my repeated failures at holiness and perfection is the hope that someday, somehow things will be different. But according to this guy, apparently not.

As Christians, we should take the accusation of hypocrisy more seriously than we do. Sure, non-Christians overuse this complaint and employ it as justification to ignore the call of Christ. But we too easily dismiss the complaint's deeper lament when we respond, "We're all sinners, right?"

I get it. I do. It's Christ that's perfect, not you. Not me.

But if we're the body of Christ, our actions shouldn't differ too greatly from his. *Who we are* should reflect Jesus. *How we live* should reveal Christ. And if it doesn't, we should ask, "Who am I granting permission to eat at my table? Christ? Or another?"

You see, confessing "I'm a sinner" is not just admitting to a mistake. It's a proclamation of union. A declaration of allegiance. An acceptance of a particular grammar disciplined under a specific master: death. Sin is "union" with death. "I'm a sinner" announces "I belong to death" or "I'm one flesh with death." It affirms a union that, given the right opportunity, provides each of us with the capacity to birth hate through the murderous pain wounding our souls. A union that disciplines us in violence, calls us toward devastation, and invites us to a dinner with hatred and unforgiveness as the main course. Through such an unholy Eucharist, transformation into death, our father, becomes complete, and the actions that follow unspeakable.

This is why Paul adamantly exhorts the Christians of Rome to break all relations with sin, to purge sin from their lives *completely*.

> Shall we go on sinning so that grace may increase? By
> no means! We are those who died to sin, so how can we
> live in it any longer? . . . Therefore do not let sin reign in
> your mortal body, obeying its evil desires. Do not offer
> any part of yourself to sin as a weapon of wickedness;
> instead, offer yourselves to God as those who have been
> brought from death to life. . . . For sin shall no longer
> be your master, because you are not under the law, but
> under grace. (Rom. 6:1–2, 12–14)

All sin is permission for someone other than God to guide us in our transformation. All sin transforms us into an image not found in Jesus. Sins, as Paul reveals, are "footholds for the devil" (Eph. 4:27) or permission to supper with Satan and whoever he invites to the meal. Thus, sin should not be embraced as central to our identity (i.e., "I'm just a sinner like you") but treated as the impostor that it is. For because we are in Christ, sin is no longer our master, and therefore, all sin must be abandoned. All un-creation emptied from ourselves to be replaced with the new creation found in Christ:

> For we know that our old self was crucified with [Jesus]
> so that the body given to sin might perish, so that we no
> longer live as slaves to sin—because whoever has died
> has been set free from sin. (Rom. 6:6–7)

Sin should have no home in the Christian, in the church, for "if anyone is in Christ, they are a new creation: The old has passed away, and behold, the new has come!" (2 Cor. 5:17).

Who have we become, then, as Christians when sin in our lives is dismissed flippantly because "Come on, we're all sinners, right?" Such an attitude harbors a fugitive of the cross that should have no place at this meal, no invitation to this dance, for in Christ we have become one with grace. Not sin. And our actions should follow.

RELEARNING HOW TO BE HUMAN

So on the path to transformation, where do *works* fit? Should they be obsessed over like the perfectionist? Or should they be cast aside like the hip I'm-just-a-sinner-like-you preacher? Or is there a third option altogether? To locate the role of *works* in the life of the Christian, we need to answer another question, one typically not asked at all: What does it mean to be human? No, not what separates us from a dolphin or a dog or a rock, but what it means to be *truly* human.

The question is birthed under the shade of the first tree of life in the garden of Eden. The question emerges from the tension that humanity was created in the image of God, who is Life, but became one flesh with death in Genesis 3 through sin, rendering humanity "subhuman." Less than what we were when we were created. So, caught in a world between two trees, what does it mean to be *truly* human? Not the distorted "subhuman" united with death, but human made in the image of God—human as one flesh with the Word-who-became-flesh.

Without question, the New Testament teaches that Jesus was fully God, but, with equal emphasis, it reveals that he was also "fully human in every way" (Heb. 2:17a). Jesus was flesh and bone; born vulnerable to death; "grew in wisdom and stature" (Luke 2:52); experienced puberty, erupted in laughter, recoiled in despair, struggled with understanding, fought off rumors, bullying, and the expectations of the crowds whose demands were more multitudinous than the masses themselves. Jesus was *truly* human, yet *without* sin.

> For we do not have a high priest who is unable to empathize with our weaknesses, but one who has been tempted in every way we are, *yet he did not sin*. (Heb. 4:15)

Human? Yes. Tempted? Indeed. Struggled with weakness? Absolutely. A sinner? Absolutely not.

Lacking sin, though, doesn't make Jesus *less* human, but *more* human than you or I have ever been. Often in our struggle with the place of works and passages revealing that "all have sinned and fallen short of the glory of God" (Rom. 3:23), we embrace the lie that sin is essential to humanity. That sin is a prerequisite to being human.

That is simply not true.

If that were the case, Adam and Eve weren't truly human until they sinned and ate the fruit, making death their true creator and God merely the assistant. No, creation preceded the Fall, preceded union with death. To be human, then, is not to sin. To sin is to be less than human.

Sin is *not* a prerequisite to be human, but evidence that we are not *truly* human at all.

Jesus was fully human and stayed fully human by abstaining from sin and remaining completely united with God—refusing the temptation to mar the image of God through "union" with death. Jesus was a second Adam who refused to follow the path of the first. Not some divine masquerade feigning struggle and suffering, deceiving us into thinking our God understands our plight. Jesus was fully human, *truly* human, precisely because he did *not* sin, even to accomplish something holy like defeating evil.

THE END NEVER JUSTIFIES THE MEANS

In Matthew 4, Jesus enters the desert to face the serpent of Eden. After fasting for forty days (emptying himself of physical desire), Jesus encounters Satan and a triad of temptations focused on Adam's folly: sin as means to God's end. "If you are the Son of God, command these stones to become bread," offering a feast to display God's provision (Matt. 4:3). "If you are the Son of God, throw yourself down," proving God's faithfulness to his beloved (Matt. 4:6). Each temptation mirroring the temptation of Adam: seize God's end (i.e., "be like God," Gen. 3:5) through death's means (i.e., "sin").

The satanic encounter climaxes in Matthew 4:8–9:

> The devil took [Jesus] to a very high mountain and showed him all the kingdoms of the world and their splendor. He said to Jesus, "I will give you all of this, if you bow down and worship me."

Satan knew why Jesus came to earth: Jesus came to establish a kingdom. This was Jesus's target; this was his goal. His Davidic genealogy announced it in Matthew 1:1, the magi proclaimed it in Matthew 2:2, John the Baptist preached it in Matthew 3:2, and Jesus himself confirms it in Matthew 4:17, "Repent, for the kingdom of heaven has come near" (NIV). Establishing the kingdom was the persistent content of his preaching,[3] for it was his goal, the intended end of his ministry, and here Satan offers it to Jesus *without* suffering, *without* death, *without* a cross—just "bow down and worship me" and all the kingdoms of the earth are yours. But Jesus knows what Adam and Eve overlooked and what our actions seem to deny: the end never justifies the means. Instead, the means define *who you are* at the end.

In *A Tale of Three Kings*, Gene Edwards depicts an explosive interaction between the fugitive King David and one of his soldiers (Joab) after David spurned the opportunity to kill King Saul in the cave recorded in 1 Samuel 24.

> Joab walked directly in front of David, looked down on him, and began roaring his frustrations.
>
> "Many times [Saul] almost speared you to death in his palace. I saw that with my own eyes. Finally, you ran away. Now for years you have been nothing but a rabbit for him to chase. Furthermore, the whole world believes the lies he tells about you. He has come—the king himself—hunting every cave, pit, and hole on earth to find you and kill you like a dog. But tonight *you* had *him* at the end of his own spear and you did nothing!
>
> "Look at us. We're animals again. Less than an hour ago you could have freed us all. Yes, we could all be free, right now! Free! And Israel, too. She would be free. Why, David? Why did you not end these years of misery?"
>
> There was a long silence. Men shifted again, uneasily. They were not accustomed to seeing David rebuked.
>
> "Because," said David very slowly (and with a gentleness that seemed to say, I heard what you asked, but not the way you asked it), . . . "Better he kill me than I learn his ways. Better he kill me than I become as he is. I shall not practice the ways that cause kings to go mad. I will not throw spears, nor will I allow hatred to grow in my heart. I will not avenge. I will not destroy the Lord's anointed. Not now. Not ever!"[4]

David understood what we often forget: the end doesn't justify the means; the means define *who you are* at the end.

This is a central message of Genesis 3. The violation in Eden was not the end ("god-likeness"), but the means by which the end was commandeered (i.e., selfish disobedience). As creation demonstrated in Genesis 1–2, our God is not a God who seizes or uses violence to attain his end. He empties himself through movements of grace toward us. Thus, the moment the fruit was seized by Adam and Eve (i.e., their "means"), humanity crossed a divine threshold of transformation, yet not of uniting with God but with death (i.e., their "end" because of their "means").

Works matter. What you do or don't do matters. Not just for salvation, but in transformation. Sin is not a prerequisite to be human; instead, sin makes you subhuman. *True* humanity, as revealed in Christ, purges all sin, never embraces sin as an ally, always refuses to partner with sin to accomplish any end, and, instead, embraces holiness and the call "to be perfect as our heavenly Father is perfect."

Rescuing Ephesians 2:8–9

Normally, around this point, our consciences rise up and we fall back into what we perceive as a clear "safe passage" from Scripture that settles all issues regarding *works* and salvation. Enter Ephesians 2:8–9:

> For you have been saved by grace through faith. And this is not from yourselves; it is the gift of God—*not by works*, so that no one can boast.

There it is. The Bible says it, I believe it, that settles it: "*Works don't matter!*"—setting down our Bibles a bit overconfident.

When pressed further ("So where do works fit?"), the typical response is something to the effect of: "Works are simply our expression of gratitude toward God for our salvation," rendering deeds to an underwhelming "thank you" for the cancellation of an infinite debt. Which is odd, given that if my wife says "I love you" with a grand expression of sacrificial love, no one would think it wise for me to respond with "Thank you." The response simply doesn't match.

But if not "thank you," then what? Where do works fit? At this point in the book, it should come as no surprise that the answer comes through the revelation of *union*—or, in this text, grace and faith as becoming-of-one-flesh.

Grace is a movement of God toward us—the unique work of God that greets us, invites us, redeems us, and offers us union with him: an invitation only possible through his initiative. For, indeed, only God's movement toward us (and not the opposite) may birth a return to our Creator, rescuing us from "union" with death. And, in Christ Jesus, he *has* moved toward us. Even while we were his enemies, he sought us, died for us, rose for us, redeemed us through his body and blood, and moved toward us yet again through the outpouring and indwelling of his Holy Spirit.

This is grace: God's ineffable movement toward us.

Faith, then, is our movement toward God—the active response of humanity to move toward the God who first moved toward us. If grace is the unique work of God, something only *God* could do, then faith is the unique work of humanity—something only *we* could do. For God is not a tyrant, overriding our will by his grace, demanding union through force or deception. Such action would render God as merely another iteration of death, for the means defines the end. Instead, like a gentle lover, God woos us, moves toward us in grace, and awaits our response—our movement back toward him.

This is faith: our movement toward God in response to his movement toward us.

This mutual movement, as Ephesians 2 points out, results in salvation—or, to define it more accurately, union. Transformation. Union between God and humanity lost in Eden but restored in Christ. A union that transforms *humanity*, for like a fire removes a metal's impurities, God cannot be approached by anyone or anything without affecting them, without purifying them, without transforming them. This union doesn't change God, but, without question, it changes us. Through this mutual movement of grace and faith, God re-creates humanity in the image of Christ, altering our logic, passions, pursuits, and, yes, even our *works*. Or, as Paul summarizes, "we are God's workmanship," God's handiwork, "created in Christ Jesus to do good works" (Eph. 2:10a NIV)—fallen humanity refashioned into *true* humanity bearing the image of God that results not in a life of sin but in a union that produces holy works of the Father.

Like sex, union with God produces fruit. Offspring. Good works.

Works, then, are not just "acts of gratitude," but the natural outworking of becoming one flesh with God, union with the Creator and sustainer of Life eternal. Works are the inevitable consequence of "God's workmanship," a natural result of Christ's atonement, an essential end for the Spirit's transformation of us by grace through faith.

TRUE HUMANITY

Thus, humanity's transformation, through Christ, into the image of God *must* result in holiness, not sin. A bachelor no longer acts as if he's single once he's wed, for union always demands corresponding action. Without the appropriate works, the union is rightly questioned; any other conclusion would be as absurd as accusing an apple tree of possessing the roots of a banana tree—for a tree is an unending, reciprocal cycle of receiving nourishment from its root that produces the bounty at the tip of its limbs. The root doesn't just give life at random, but it gives a *specific* life consistent with the type of tree it actually is. And by grace through faith, our root is Christ, so our works should reflect his.

1 John 2:6 puts it simply, "Whoever claims to live in Christ must walk just as Jesus walked." Must live as Jesus lived. Must say what Jesus said. Must do what Jesus did. Must follow wherever Jesus leads. For as the "firstborn from the dead," Christ unveils sin as an impostor, not holiness. Sin leads to "union" with death, but holiness leads to *true* humanity—union with God in Christ. Christians, therefore, are God's workmanship, created in Christ Jesus to do the works of Christ, that flow from Christ, and lead back to Christ.

As Christians, we should confidently say with Paul, "Imitate me as I imitate Christ" (1 Cor. 11:1). Yet most of us shy away from this verse with apprehension. "What, me? Follow *me* as I follow Christ? No—follow Jesus, not *me*." On the surface, this response sounds holy, but in reality it's quite appalling. If people follow you and don't end at Christ, then where are *you* headed? What are *you* connected to? Who are *you* following? Our connection with the root of Christ should be so secure that tracing our tracks should lead straight to the feet of Jesus. If not, then change paths and follow Jesus up the Via Dolorosa. For sin is only produced through "union" with death, yet union with Christ is union with Life—and our deeds are sure to follow if the connection is secure.

Grace is God's movement toward us, and *faith* is our movement toward God. Mutual movements that result in union that produces *works*. Works employed by the Holy Spirit to move, yet again, toward the world—through us. Becoming one flesh with God transforms our lives (deeds, words, worship, all of it) into a movement of God toward the ends of the earth, so that, like priests, we become a tangible bridge to the intangible. Through our union with God, a bodily presence of Christ is experienced by the world, compelling them toward the mystery of God through the grace he extends. Thus, works are not just evidence of justification, but an avenue for cosmic transformation begotten through divine union.

Or, as Paul states it, by grace through faith, we become the "body of Christ" (1 Cor. 12:27).

THE PERFECT TRANSFORMATION

I don't begin this journey holy and perfect, but I follow Christ closely on the road *he* paved to our heavenly Father. I follow him on my road to Damascus, where I encounter the Word of God through fear and trembling, blinding me to the world, yet opening my eyes to a new creation. A new existence. A new identity. A new definition of "perfect."

The call to be "holy as God is holy" is not to be ignored, feared, or engaged as an incarceration with legalistic zeal or flippantly cast aside as a vile distortion of the gospel of faith alone. Instead, passages like Matthew 5:48 or 1 Peter 1:16 or Ephesians 2:8–10 invite us to reenter the womb anew, to dislodge ourselves from "union" with death, to engage *true* humanity in the image of God wed to God. In other words, "perfection" (or *true* humanity) is walking as Jesus did on a path paved with patience and grace.

CHAPTER SIXTEEN

EATING FROM THE TREE OF LIFE
Union with the God Who Pursues

The Bible ends where it begins: in a garden, with the tree of life. Yet not with the shadow of death eclipsing the sun. Not with the cold chill of the thought that "all is lost." The Bible ends with *union* and a *divine word*.

> And then I saw a new heaven and a new earth, for the
> first heaven and the first earth had passed away . . . And
> I saw the Holy City, the new Jerusalem, coming down
> out of heaven from God, having been prepared as a
> bride beautifully adorned for her husband. (Rev. 21:1–2)

Heaven and earth now together. Heaven and earth now "one flesh." Now united, sharing the same space, so that the abode of God and the abode of man are *truly* one. Heaven and earth coming together, so that while distinctions remain, union is complete, for "the dwelling place of God is now with humanity. He will dwell with them, and they will be his people. God himself will be with them and be their God" (Rev. 21:3).

No more division. No more curse. Just *union*. Union and a *divine word* that provides indescribable healing:

And he will wipe every tear from their eyes. And there
will be no more death or mourning or crying or pain,
for the old order of things has passed away. (Rev. 21:4)

There may be no picture more tender than God wiping away the
tears from our eyes. Tears of lingering pain, tears of anxiety wondering "Is this a dream?" Tears of relief knowing that life is no
longer lived between two trees, but under the shade of the tree of
life cascading with leaves of healing (Rev. 22:2b). Tears that God
wipes away along with old creation, and, like the words from the
cross, announces over renewed Eden a *divine word*: "It is done"
(Rev. 21:6).

It is finished.

The Divine Mystery of Communication

When we engage words, we engage something sacred. Something
divine. Something holy and shrouded in mystery. For words carry
meaning, carry hope, carry transformation, carry endless pursuit.
Words carry the burden of communication.

Communication is a transcendent mystery on the level of
love, the meaning of life, or even salvation itself. Communication
defies logic, definition, and ascends to realms of beauty far beyond
earthly creation. Like a plastic bag in the wind, communication
at times scurries across the ground with clear touches to the
earth, yet immediately rises in the air, suspended in the heavens. Language flits between the literal and the figurative without
warning, because the goal is larger than following the rules of a
particular category. The goal is communication. And communication is a vast ocean of mystery, with riptides, rolling waves,
destructive tsunamis, and cavernous depths beyond what human
inventions can explore for fear of being crushed under its weight.

Communication is verbal, yet essentially nonverbal—both vying for the premier position from moment to moment. Posture communicates, tone communicates, word order communicates, raised eyebrows communicate, and so does the furrowed brow. Slouching communicates, shifting eyes communicate, and so does a piercing gaze. Quickness communicates as much as a saunter. Words on a page communicate and so do monotone meandering sermons. Musical notes communicate and so do zeroes and ones. Communication occurs whether words are present or not. A static painting in a silent gallery can speak more words than a seasoned lecturer, because every stroke of the brush intends to communicate. To pull from the heavenly realm messages barely divined by earth's inhabitants.

Yet by God's grace, communication also uses words, even while it never desires to stay within them. Like all things physical, words are limitations of *true* reality so that the physical can interact with the nonphysical. Like a tree or sex or a sublime dessert, physical limitations are created as conduits through which we can interact with the divine. Divine communication, by its very nature, extends beyond words to elevate us to the presence of that which cannot be contained in creation, thoughts, or human utterances. Yet this doesn't trivialize words; it clarifies them, exalts them. Transforms all physical existence into a movement of grace where the divine can be approached by his creation. Approached by the creature caught in a world between two trees simply looking for a place to belong.

Humanity's Pursuit

Belonging. What a strange idea. Oftentimes we chameleon our way into situations and settings with the sole intent to belong. To belong to something bigger than us. To belong to something other than us. To belong to something that gives us purpose, meaning, or the reminder that we matter. Belonging is something we all pursue, even if we do so by running in the opposite direction. Belonging is something we've even transformed into a descriptor for our prized possessions that bring us comfort: "our *belonging*s." To be claimed by someone or something embraces our heart in ways that possessions can only dream of and Hollywood only pretends.

Not long ago, my wife sat across from me in our living room and said, "I finally realized after fourteen years of marriage the reason I struggle with confrontation. The reason I hate even simple arguments with you." With tears in her eyes and her lip bouncing about, "In the back of my mind," she continued, "deep down in my heart I wonder, 'Will this be it? Will this be the argument that finally pushes Shane away? Will this be what causes you to leave me like everyone else in my life?'"

I was dumbfounded. We'd been married over fourteen years with no indication of anything other than forever. A bit broken, I asked her, "What did I do to make you think *that*?"

She shook her head and said, "Nothing . . . I think that's what I fear about *everyone* that's close to me. I just never realized it until now."

You see, when my wife was eight, her mom left her and her brothers for another man, and in many ways, my wife has been searching for her mom ever since. Sure, they talk; we even go visit on occasion. But a chasm opened between them on that day thirty years ago that is yet to be healed—yet to be bridged in the heart of my wife. A chasm between my wife and her mom, but also between my wife and *belonging*.

We pursue belonging with such zeal, we're willing to categorize and recategorize ourselves, going to whatever lengths necessary to feel the elusive embrace of belonging. Some cling to sexual orientation, others to womanizing, others to religion, others to power, others to votes, others to perversion—whatever it takes, whatever the means, so long as the end is belonging.

Belonging is a desperate plea in our souls and a risk unlike any other. Exposed like the homeless person on the corner holding a sign, willing to take whatever someone will give, even just a smile instead of a look of rejection or recoil. Putting yourself out there with the request, "Will you take me? Do I belong?" is dangerous. The risk is so great, the vulnerability so daunting, often we'd rather run into the arms of death than face the obstacles of belonging. For belonging is betrothed to trust and interwoven with love, cycling us in a spiral of desire and fear, of longing and hiding, of desperation and panic.

And so we wander. From place to place, step to step, hoping to stumble upon belonging yet fearing confinement to endless *searching*.

Now, don't get me wrong, searching does come with an air of adventure. To search for meaning, to search for love, to search for treasures, or the right word for a sentence or the right chord for a song can be as exhilarating as the destination itself. That is, of course, until we can't find what we're looking for no matter how much effort we exert—our keys when we're late for a meeting, our Chapstick we're sure we left on the night stand, our minds as we navigate and negotiate the needs and emotions of our children. Searching carries with it a strain and a chaos as misplacement turns frantic, rapidly turning the search from bliss to blunder, from joy to tribulation. As the frenzy increases, our understanding declines, and in frustration, searching quickly turns into desperation—and the more treasured the prize, the greater the spiral spins out of control.

We search so intently at times we even forget what we're looking for.

Humanity's Amnesia

Between two trees, it's easy to forget.

It's easy to forget childlike wonder. It's easy to misplace divine gifts. It's easy to fight for ourselves, to embrace the lie that we can't be different, that we can't change, that we're all alone and there's no hope. It's easy to forget there's more to the story than just the dragon's fury; there's more to the story than just evil's victory. There's more to the story than despair, suffering, loneliness, and trials.

Between two trees, it's easy to forget: we're searching for belonging. We're searching for the intimacy of Eden. We're searching for the belonging loudly proclaimed by all of creation.

We often forget creation teems with communication, both verbal and nonverbal.

I'm writing this chapter in a unique space I intentionally sought out because I knew it would ignite something deep within me: the Athenaeum library in Providence, Rhode Island. It's not very big, although the mounds of books lining every square inch may obscure the true size of this space. But, like many places, what I envisioned was quite different: something a bit more dignified, elaborate, marble-laden with scents of inspiration emanating from the fresh preservation of the distant past. I mean, this was the building frequently graced by H. P. Lovecraft. This was the writing space of Edgar Allan Poe where he courted the poet Sarah Helen Whitman just a year before his death. This is a space filled with busts of Benjamin Franklin, Julius Caesar, and other ghosts from the past still, in some mystical sense, claiming a presence. This is a space teeming with communication.

Sitting in such a storied space reminds me of the moving moments I had walking the streets of Ephesus in modern-day Turkey. My feet impressing the same ground as Paul, Timothy, and John the apostle. My space intersecting with their space, only separated by something as trivial as time. Something stirs in me in moments like these. Something far beneath the surface moving at a supernatural pace. I guess, in many ways, what I'm describing is revelation. Communication. A movement of grace in which we unite with something far removed from creation. A union between the space of God and the space of man. An Eden.

Between two trees, it's easy to forget that space is more than just space. Creation is more than just matter; it's an entry point for divine union. When God created "space" in Genesis 1, it was a movement of grace that limits (i.e., all things take up space) in order to provide interaction with the limitless. For God chose to communicate his love, his truth, his life, his grace to humanity in the physical realm. In creation.

This is why Jesus's death leads to a bodily resurrection. His resurrection reminds us of the value and worth of creation. When Christ died on the cross, he wasn't judging the physical realm, he was restoring it. He wasn't condemning the material world as unworthy of the divine, a prison to overcome, a hindrance to endure until the true spiritual reality could replace the wretched shadow of physical creation. The cross leads to a resurrection of the *physical* body revealing Christ's purpose to reunify creation with the divine. Christ's resurrection rends the veil between heaven and earth, uniting the Creator with his creation.

Before the Fall, creation was a movement of grace where humanity conversed with divinity through its space. And today, between two trees, "creation groans," longing to return to its position of glory as a bridge between humanity and God, a priest of sorts that connects creature to Creator. Creation understands its origin, delights in its purpose, and longs to return to its prior form.

Twenty minutes sitting on the front porch bears witness to creation's vocation: birds whistle melodious meditations, winds wisp eager to visit new people and places, insects subtly talk at a level only audible when they buzz close by our ear, sprouts yawn stretching toward the sun, as fruit sighs with delight as it is consumed by animals and humans alike. Even *our* creations within creation mimic their creator with a cadence and a commitment to unite with the rest of the earth: cars pass by embraced by the wind, creating sounds that crescendo and decrescendo, while the pavement beneath bends with a slight smile to support the weight of its transient visitor. Clouds communicate with passing parodies of creation in fluent shapes, while the blueness of the sky recedes in places to make room for birds in flight and planes in transit.

Creation communicates. Creation bears witness. Creation sings different melodies but participates in the same symphony: a song of Eden that celebrates the fallen world's search for belonging. Our *search* for true, unconditional *belonging* only found in God. The same God, we've forgotten, who's been searching for us this whole time.

The God Who Pursues

Between two trees, it's easy to forget that our God is a God who pursues. Recklessly. Relentlessly. Furiously pursues. Not just *some* of creation. *All* of creation.

And yet, it's easy to forget—even when the entire Bible sings this message, starting with the opening lyrics: "In the beginning, God created." In the beginning, God moved toward us. In the beginning, God needed nothing, but he chose to create you, he chose to create me, and, incredibly, he chose to create us *in his image* (Gen. 1:26–27). Why? Because our God is a God who pursues.

And the pursuit didn't end after the Fall in Genesis 3. As we hid behind our fig leaves, "united" with death, traveling east of Eden, God didn't abandon us or avoid us like the elusive deities in the pagan pantheons. He pursued us. When we built Babel in Genesis 11, God called Abraham to bless all nations in Genesis 12. When we grumbled in the desert in Exodus 16, God gave us bread from heaven and water from a rock in Exodus 17. God moved toward us through his law in Exodus 20. And God moved toward us through his prophets in Isaiah 1.

Why? Because our God is a God who pursues.

When we were without direction, he sent us judges; when we were without options, he immobilized the sun; when we were without hope, he became flesh and dwelled among us. Time and again, God moves toward us to redeem us, to unite with us, to return us to Eden. Whether we're talking about the tabernacle or the temple, the Exodus or the Exile, the incarnation or the out-pouring of the Holy Spirit, over and over and over in Scripture one thing is clear: our God is a God who pursues.

Persistently. Passionately. Shattering barriers, crossing bound-aries, interpenetrating heaven and earth to unleash his love on us. To restore us. To transform us. To be *with* us.

Between two trees, life is hard. Life is lonely. Life is a struggle. A struggle with time and space that suffocates any life bold enough to linger, any hope brazen enough to lumber on, any faith auda-cious enough to challenge confusion, fight disillusion, or believe in a resurrection. A yoke so excessive it's as if death itself were alive, prowling about like a roaring lion, waiting for just the right moment to overwhelm the unaware and overturn the ill-prepared. Between two trees, life is lived in the shadow of the tree of death. We all know it. We all feel it. We're just powerless to overcome it.

And so we search for belonging; we desire transformation, longing to be someone different. Even though we try to avoid it, even though we try to suppress it, even though we try to ignore, mock, and forget it, this longing in our hearts never goes away. Even if it changes shape the older we get, this longing to be some-one different, this longing to transform never disappears. Why? Because it's a gift from God. A gift from the God who pursues.

You see, our adventures as children were not just exercises in fantasy or silly explorations of impossible worlds. Instead, they're evidence of God's pursuit and our desire to return to him. Our desire to return to our Creator. To transform into the image of the One who lovingly and tenderly created us and moves toward us. And even though Genesis 3 launched us into a world between two trees, our God still calls to us. He still beckons us. He still pursues us. Not through shame. Not through guilt. But through grace. And when we see this clearly, we may start to see ourselves as *he* sees us—a child worthy of pursuit.

God's Word between Two Trees

I think English made the right choice with the word *communication*, embedding the word "communion" within it. For communication is about union, an attempt at oneness. A movement of grace in a divine word.

With the Word, God speaks and worlds fall into place with rationalities, creativity, and infinite exploration embedded in their potentiality. When God speaks, the Word becomes flesh and dwells among us (John 1:14), growing in stature and wisdom (Luke 2:52), walking to and fro, longing for love, laughing at idiocy, and genuinely embracing the mysterious complexities of the people around him. This is why we were not just created *through* the Word, but we exist and are sustained *by* the Word—we live not on "bread alone" but on the very Word of God (Matt. 4:4).

And our God never stops talking.

If he did, our universe would collapse on itself, for we are held together by words from the Word. Thus, the essential end of transformation is not arriving at a singular destination, but submerging ourselves in the mystery of the ever-creating Trinity who is making all things new. Kind of like interpreting the Bible. We approach Scripture, the Word-become-page, the same way we approach Christ, the Word-become-flesh. Not as a warden looking to acquire yet another occupant for the cells of our own creation, but as a prisoner of death's deception willing and able to admit "I don't know." Submitting and surrendering to God's creative communication.

Communication, like creation, is a gift. An invitation. A constant call from the beyond that rains down a thousand different ways to pronounce the same word: "Come."

> Come, all you who are thirsty, and I will give drink
> from the springs of the water of life. Come, all you who
> are weak and weary, all you who are poor and broken.
> Come to the foot of the cross so you can come to Life.
> So you can unite with the Creator himself.

In the beginning, the Father created by gently whispering "Come." The Word became flesh and cried out in the dark void: "Come." The Spirit descended on the repentant with a resounding "Come." The apostles speak with the invitation to "Come." The prophets say "Come." The law says "Come." The bride says "Come." And John ends the Bible with a message to the world caught between two trees that mirrors the words of the crucified King: "Come. *Come, Lord Jesus.*"

And so, I end this book the same way: "Come." *Come* receive the divine. *Come* to the cross to empty your baggage and burdens, picking up a cross of your own. *Come,* pass through the empty tomb to a new life birthed in the womb of the grave. *Come,* open your eyes to the Spirit, indwelling and guiding you to salvation and Sabbath, transformation and union, the Father and the Lamb.

You with eyes to see and ears to hear: *Come.*

You who do evil and *you* who do good, *you* in poverty and *you* in prosperity, *you* with wounds and *you* with hatred, *you* with unforgiveness and *you* with pain unimaginable: *Come.*

Return to the God in whose image you were fashioned, in the beginning. Just *Come*.

Embrace the tree between two trees, the cross of Calvary, and emerge from the empty tomb with scars on your hands and your side that celebrate immeasurable healing, divine transformation, and union with the triune God.

Simply *come*.

Acknowledgments

I am grateful. Humbled as I write this page to reflect on the good gifts of the people that surround me, not just in a time of writing a book, but on a daily basis, giving the support, rebuke, and encouragement I need to simply *be*. It is essential, therefore, in light of God's grace and the message of this book for me to offer gratitude to this cloud of saints who make up my community, from which this book is but one small fruit.

I'm so thankful for the place I work. At Ozark Christian College, I get to witness firsthand servant leaders who pour themselves out like Mary, the Mother of God, and invest in students who teach me more about Christ than any of my lectures could hope. Thanks Matt Proctor and Doug Aldridge for creating space for me to explore the depths of God and encouraging me along the way. Thanks to the students who took time to read this entire manuscript, offering insights and reflections of their heart that I treasure: Josh Gregor, Shelby Ingalls, Jordan Keller, Kyla Marlin, Samuel Parker, Blake Pesetzky, Flint Spencer, Mariah Tachick, Michelle Weeks, and Kathlyn Wieland.

Leafwood Publishers has simply been a delight to work with. Jason Fikes, you believed in this book long before I did myself. You persistently demonstrated to me patience and confidence, regardless of how I was being thrown about on the waves of the ocean. You invested in me without absolute certainty of what finished product you would receive. I am truly grateful for your humility and grace. Rebecka Scott, your leadership, managing the process from the uneven manuscript to the polished final product, was invigorating. Your excitement and dedication to this project humbling. Your commitment to the Lord life-giving. I also want to thank Duane Anderson, Lettie Morrow, and the whole team at Leafwood. I don't deserve your generous efforts, but I will treasure them all the same.

Don Gates, I'm truly thankful for your steadfast endurance. You are more than an agent for me, my friend. You are a wise guide with a heart surrendered to the Lord. You have been unwavering in your commitment to me, confident in the gifts I could not see. Thank you for sharing your vision and your care.

For me, writing takes a unique combination of conversation partners, familial care, and unique getaways. Thank you, Steve and Michelle Meyer, for graciously offering your lake house as I fumbled through the latter portions of the writing process, and forgive me, Alexis, my wonderful sister-in-law, for invading your northeastern home with my family of six as your husband gallivanted across Germany learning the language on BC's dime. You and your sweet girls were such a gift to us in those two weeks.

Jessica Scheuermann, more than just a conversation partner, you read every word, from the drivel to the jewels, counseling me and my insecurities while teaching me how to find my voice in writing. I'm truly indebted to you. And grateful all the more.

Doug Welch, thank you for patiently listening to me as I rambled through half-baked chapters on end, promising to take up only ten minutes of your time while you graciously carved out an hour or more each time. I'm truly thankful for the rich and free discussions you afford.

Three more names come to mind when I think of the laborious process of crafting this book. Originally, I wrote forty to fifty separate essays that were rearranged, rewritten, and even removed to mold the semblance of coherence found in the sixteen chapters of this book. I could not do that on my own, for quite often I felt blinded by my own words. Yet, the painstaking work of Tim Morgan (my research assistant, second to none), Jordan Wood (my brother, whose mind is second to none), and Thomas Williams (my developing editor and now friend) brought this sculpture from the block of marble. Indeed, all of the mistakes herein are mine alone, but any accolades thereafter must be shared with them. Thank you, gentlemen.

Finally, my family. Our home group (whom my children refer to as aunts, uncles, and cousins) is a constant source of strength. Each of you in your own way encouraged and propelled me forward, sustaining me through your presence, patience, and love. I'm so grateful to have a community that shows me what triune love *is* in this world between two trees.

My Mom and Dad, to whom I dedicate this work, I am so thankful for you. You brought me into this world through love, and nurtured me along with patience fit for a canonical character. You introduced me to Jesus, and, like Mary, urged me forward to union with God through tears and laughter. Earthly parents that resemble our heavenly father are rare—and so I treasure the gems you are.

My wonderful wife Sara and my four incredible kids: Zion, Paige, Maddox, and Robert. Who am I without you? You are daily reminders of God's grace. Triune gifts housed in my home, tolerant of my quirks, patient with my transformation, and a constant source of spiritual growth. I learn from you. I live life with you. I am better because of you. Thanks for being my mirror. Thanks for being Jesus to me. Thanks for being love incarnate in this journey between two trees. I love you.

NOTES

CHAPTER ONE: THE WAGES OF SIN
[1]Book 9, lines 780–84.

CHAPTER TWO: THE DEPTHS OF UNION
[1]See also Jeremiah 15:16. Cf. Jeremiah 20:9.

[2]A detailed examination of the solution (or the answer to the question: "How did God respond to the Fall?") begins in Chapter Seven: "Our Father Remains: Beauty and the Tree of Life." The present discussion, as indicated by the title of this chapter ("The Depths of Union: Becoming One Flesh with Death"), is focused on demonstrating the severity of the problem from Genesis 3.

CHAPTER THREE: DARKNESS FEARING THE LIGHT
[1]Plato, *Apology* 38a, 5–6.

[2]My explanatory paraphrase.

[3]Trevor W. Thompson, "Paul and the Jaws of Death (1 Cor. 15:32): Animals and the Pathology of Illness" (unpublished paper; presented at Society of Biblical Literature Conference, San Antonio, TX, November 19, 2016).

[4]Johannes P. Louw and Eugene A. Nida, eds., *Greek-English Lexicon of the New Testament: Based on Semantic Domains,* 2nd ed. (New York: American Bible Society, 1989), 79.43. Emphasis added.

CHAPTER FOUR: LIFE IN THE SHADOWS
[1]The opening lines of the Declaration of Independence.

[2]The narrated exchange and subsequent quotes are from G. M. Gilbert, *Nuremberg Diary* (New York: Farrar, Strauss, and Company, 1947), 278–79.

[3]Matthew 28:5; Luke 1:13, 30; 2:10.

[4]Isaiah 8:12; 41:10, 13; 43:1; Jeremiah 10:5; Zephaniah 3:16; Haggai 2:5.

[5]Matthew 14:27; 17:7; Mark 5:36; Luke 5:10; Revelation 1:17.

CHAPTER FIVE: THE STATE OF OUR UNION
[1]Genesis 1:26, "And then God said, 'Let us make humanity in our image, according to our likeness . . .'"

[2]See Chapters Seven through Nine for a more detailed discussion of "union with God."

[3]See also Mark 9:33–35.

[4] For a more detailed discussion of the cross, see Chapter Seven, "Our Father Remains: Beauty and the Tree of Life," and Chapter Eight, "'It Is Finished': Embracing Death to Find Life."

CHAPTER SIX: SEPARATE WE STAND

[1] Lionel Robbins, *An Essay on the Nature and Significance of Economic Science* (London: Macmillan, 1932), 15.

[2] Genesis 1:4, 10, 12, 18, 21, 25, 31.

[3] See also Revelation 13:12, 14.

[4] All passages in this paragraph are from the NIV, 2011.

[5] So, for example, in Plato's *Symposium* 178e3–179b6, Phaedrus suggests homosexual love (in a context of commitment) would encourage a superior army in that "For a man in love would surely choose to have all the rest of the host [perish] rather than his favourite," a motivation capable of making "even a little band victorious over all the world." Plato, *Lysis, Symposium, Gorgias*, trans. and ed. W. R. M. Lamb, Loeb Classical Library 166 (Cambridge, MA: Harvard University Press, 1925), 103.

[6] Genesis 3:5, "God knows that when you eat . . . *you will be like God*, knowing good and evil."

CHAPTER EIGHT: "IT IS FINISHED"

[1] Cf. Luke 23:40–43 (not found in Matthew, Mark, or John).

[2] My paraphrase.

[3] For more discussion, see Chapter One, "The Wages of Sin: It's Worse Than Hell," and Chapter Two, "The Depths of Union: Becoming One Flesh with Death" above.

[4] See figure on p. 121.

[5] Significantly, this event occurs in Cana, which, as John reminds, is "where [Jesus] had turned the water into wine" (John 4:46a NIV).

[6] See Chapter Two, "The Depths of Union: Becoming One Flesh with Death," pp. 37–38.

[7] See Chapter Five, "The State of Our Union: Divided We Fall," pp. 68–71. Due to Christ's revelation of Death's deception, for the remainder of the book "Death" will no longer be capitalized but will be rendered "death."

[8] Notice the pervasiveness of union intimated in the ingestion of liquid from the cup of death (cf. the Lord's Supper).

[9] Matthew 27:50–53, "When, again, Jesus had cried out in a loud voice, he gave up his spirit. . . . The earth shook, the rocks split, and *the tombs broke open*. The bodies of many saints who had died *were raised to life*. And they *came out from the tombs* after Jesus' resurrection . . ."

[10] I'm indebted to Justin Gill, a former student of mine, for this connection. I find our conversations quite fruitful and thought-provoking. Indeed, a gift.

CHAPTER NINE: SEX

[1] *Dio Cassius* 62.28.2–3.

[2] Leviticus 18:6–23; 19:20; 20:10–21; Jeremiah 7:9; Matthew 5:27–30; Romans 1:26–31; 1 Corinthians 6:9–10; Galatians 5:19–21; Colossians 3:5–7; Hebrews 12:14–16, 13:4; 1 Peter 4:1–4; Revelation 2:20.

Chapter Ten: Opening the Womb to Truth

[1] See Chapter Eight, "'It Is Finished': Embracing Death to Find Life," pp. 118–19.

Chapter Eleven: Permission

[1] Kershaw graciously published this work that synthesizes his two-volume work on Hitler, for which he was knighted in 2002 for his service to historical research on World War II.

[2] It is important to note that 1 Corinthians 12 flows out of a conversation on the Lord's Supper in 1 Corinthians 11:17–34.

Chapter Twelve: Wishing Away the Day

[1] Irenaeus (AD 130–202) was a disciple of Polycarp, who had been a disciple of the apostle John (*Against Heresies* 3.3.4).

[2] *Against Heresies* 4.38.4. See also 3.16.7.

[3] My imaginative paraphrase.

Chapter Thirteen: The Place of Pain

[1] C. S. Lewis, *The Problem of Pain* (1940; repr., San Francisco: Harper, 2001), 91.

Chapter Fifteen: True Humanity

[1] Martin Luther, *Luther's Works*, vol. 39, ed. Eric W. Gritsch and Helmut T. Lehmann (St. Louis, MO: Concordia, 1963), 399.

[2] So, for instance, Revelation 3:1b–2 says, "I know your *deeds*. You have a reputation of being alive, but you are dead. Wake up! Strengthen what remains and is about to die, for I have not found your *deeds* complete in the eyes of my God." Or also, Revelation 20:12 says, "And I saw the dead, both great and small, standing before the throne, and books were opened. Another book was opened, which is the book of life. The dead were judged *according to the things they had done* as recorded in the books." See also Matthew 7:16–20; 21:43; Luke 6:43–45; Revelation 2:2, 19; 3:8, 15; 14:13.

[3] Matthew 4:23; 5:3, 10; 6:9–10, 33; 7:21; 8:10–12; 9:35; 10:7; 11:11–15; 12:25–28; 13:10–12, 18–23, 24, 31, 33, 37–43, 44–46, 47–50, 52; 16:19, 28; 18:1–5; 20:1–16; 21:31b–32, 43–44; 23:13; 25:1–13, 34–46; 26:29.

[4] Gene Edwards, *A Tale of Three Kings: A Study in Brokenness* (Carol Stream, IL: Tyndale, 1980), 35–36.

Scripture Index